Y0-DFI-447

Self-Made Maverick

*Break Free of
Conventional
Business Wisdom
for Lasting Success*

Dr. Reza Zahedi

GREENLEAF
BOOK GROUP PRESS

This publication is designed to provide accurate and authoritative information in regard to the subject matter covered. It is sold with the understanding that the publisher and author are not engaged in rendering legal, accounting, or other professional services. Nothing herein shall create an attorney-client relationship, and nothing herein shall constitute legal advice or a solicitation to offer legal advice. If legal advice or other expert assistance is required, the services of a competent professional should be sought.

Published by Greenleaf Book Group Press
Austin, Texas
www.gbgpress.com

Copyright © 2025 Reza Zahedi

All rights reserved.

Thank you for purchasing an authorized edition of this book and for complying with copyright law. No part of this book may be reproduced, stored in a retrieval system, used for training artificial intelligence technologies or systems, or transmitted by any means, electronic, mechanical, photocopying, recording, or otherwise, without written permission from the copyright holder.

Distributed by Greenleaf Book Group

For ordering information or special discounts for bulk purchases, please contact Greenleaf Book Group at PO Box 91869, Austin, TX 78709, 512.891.6100.

Design and composition by Greenleaf Book Group
Cover design by Greenleaf Book Group and John van der Woude

Publisher's Cataloging-in-Publication data is available.

Print ISBN: 979-8-88645-402-4

eBook ISBN: 979-8-88645-403-1

To offset the number of trees consumed in the printing of our books, Greenleaf donates a portion of the proceeds from each printing to the Arbor Day Foundation. Greenleaf Book Group has replaced over 50,000 trees since 2007.

Printed in the United States of America on acid-free paper

25 26 27 28 29 30 31 32   10 9 8 7 6 5 4 3 2 1

First Edition

To my mum, Tara, for teaching me the power of questioning everything and challenging the status quo. Your wisdom and guidance have shaped me into a true Maverick—unafraid to think differently, take risks, and build my own path to success. This is a reflection of everything you've instilled in me.

Contents

Introduction 1

   1: To Hell with "Normal" 7

   2: Zero Is the New Million 19

   3: Expect the Unexpected 33

   4: Nurture Rules Nature 49

   5: Grit over Luck 61

   6: Mastering Money: Control Wealth, Command Freedom 79

   7: No Team, No Dream 91

   8: Learning Never Stops: Adapt or Die 109

   9: The Power of No: Command Your Time,
             Dominate Your Life 131

  10: Fail Fast, Learn Faster 147

  11: Success Is the Easy Part 165

Conclusion 183

Reflection Questions 187

Acknowledgments 191

About the Author 193

Introduction

Let's cut to the chase and get right to the reason you bought this book: to build your empire. If you thought that reading the introduction would be a shortcut to getting all the information in this book, then you should put it down and buy a different one. There's no magic pill to achieving your goals. Because without hard work and, yes, failing sometimes, you won't get anywhere.

You might be wondering why you should listen to me. What makes me qualified to guide you through the unpredictable journey of entrepreneurship?

I didn't come from money. My first job was delivering newspapers, then flipping burgers for minimum wage at Burger King. But through relentless effort, unconventional thinking, and a refusal to follow the beaten path, I built multiple seven-figure businesses from scratch, scaling struggling companies to profitability and securing multimillion-dollar deals. I've mentored more than one hundred entrepreneurs, helping them navigate challenges, build resilience, and create real success.

Beyond my own ventures, I've helped start-ups break through plateaus, advised businesses on adapting to disruptive market trends, and built a mentorship program that has changed the trajectory of countless entrepreneurs. I don't just teach theories—I've lived every lesson in this book.

This isn't about following conventional business wisdom; it's about breaking the rules, thinking differently, and creating your own opportunities. That's exactly what I've done, and that's exactly what I'm going to teach you how to do.

―

On my eighteenth birthday, I was hoping to get a car, or at least a bike. Instead, my mother handed me three books: the Bible, the Torah, and the Koran.

"Now you can decide whatever you want to believe, Reza," she told me.

This statement meant a lot coming from her. You see, my mother was born and raised in a Muslim country, where giving your son books from other religions wasn't exactly conventional. At age twenty, when she moved to the Netherlands with me, she found herself in a Christian-based refugee camp. She started going to church on Sundays and took a strong liking to this new religion. Watching her make bold choices like this for herself, even when they went against the grain, taught me that I had the power to change my life at any given moment.

Mom also taught me to question everything I saw and heard. She taught me that until I knew something to be true for myself, it was only a myth. This type of contrarian thinking has made me more resilient, more confident, and more successful in life and in business than most people my age. It's helped me weather storms that look like tornadoes to others. It's helped me see opportunity on paths that to others seem like dead ends. Mostly, having a contrarian mindset has helped me get clear on what my own set of truths is.

This book is like my own "bible" to guide you through the principles behind the way I conduct my professional and personal life. In each chapter, I'll address my own contrarian truths versus the common conventional routes that most entrepreneurs are taught to follow. I'll also give you exercises to start thinking like a contrarian yourself so that, eventually, you can find your own truths.

> **She taught me that until I knew something to be true for myself, it was only a myth. This type of contrarian thinking has made me more resilient, more confident, and more successful in life and in business than most people my age.**

We live in a world where things change by the day, by the hour, and even by the minute. With the advent of AI, many jobs are already becoming obsolete. Truck drivers, office workers, factory workers, medical assistants, marketers, and people across every field will have to adapt more and more to the changing times if they want to remain relevant. They'll have to learn new skills and essentially reinvent themselves. This is where the contrarian mindset comes into the game.

I'd say the path ahead can be daunting, but that would be a lie. The truth is, as you may already suspect, there is no path. As entrepreneurs, we must carve our own route to get to where we're going by creating our own luck. And that route changes often. Why? Because our destination is unique, and it, too, can change. Our definition of success is ever evolving, based on our shifting values and perspectives. Because of this, we often feel alone and unsure of where to put our foot down next.

> **As entrepreneurs, we must carve our own route to get to where we're going by creating our own luck.**

As fellow trailblazers, we do, however, all have something in common: drive. I share that same fire in the belly that every entrepreneur has. And I, too, once had the same burning questions that you do. How do I know? Because before I wrote a single word in this book, I sat down with many of the people I mentor, asking what people like you wanted to know. Here are just some of the most pressing questions shared:

- How do I stay motivated amid constant setbacks?
- What strategic decisions can I make to ensure that my business grows?
- How do I build resilience to face inevitable challenges?
- How do I withstand the criticism of others?
- What measures can I take to make my business sustainable?
- What are the downsides to success?
- How do I combat negative self-talk?
- What's the one book every young entrepreneur should read?

That last question I'll answer right now. If you're a young entrepreneur just starting out, this book is the only compass you'll need to navigate the complexities of building your own business from the ground up.

Each chapter of this book addresses a myth that traditional-minded businesspeople believe versus the truth that a contrarian entrepreneur knows from experience. With real-life examples from my own failures and successes, I'll provide actionable solutions to the challenges you face. It's the book I wish I had had when I was first starting out, working for minimum wage at Burger King. It's the book I'll hand my own kids when I have them.

I didn't write this because I believe I have discovered the exact formula for success—that would be naive. As I've already said, each person's course is unique, just as my own journey has been. As an Iranian immigrant raised by a single mother, I could have easily fallen through the cracks. But with hard work, creative thinking, and a bit of luck (that I made myself), I managed to turn each of those cracks into loopholes and shift the reality of my future.

The code outlined in this book has been the foundation of my success, and I am passionate about sharing it with you. By the end of the book, you will understand that success is not a straight path but a journey filled with challenges, learning, and growth. *Self-Made Maverick: Break Free of Conventional Business Wisdom for Lasting Success* will help you develop your own tools to pave your own way in a changing world.

You'll discover the profound impact that a positive, long-term mindset has on your external surroundings and how to cultivate more of it to attract positive outcomes in your business and personal life. This was the first and most crucial lesson I learned when I started out in business. You'll also learn how to think outside the box and view each failure as a powerful learning opportunity. With this in mind, you'll develop skills to help you master the art of resilience each time you encounter a setback.

We'll focus on your big-picture goals, and I'll help you define what success means to you individually, both on a professional and personal level. Next, I'll help you build a unique set of metrics to measure that success. You'll learn practical skills you can apply right away, including how to do the following:

- Make strategic decisions that align with your long-term goals
- Identify hidden opportunities based on thorough research and analysis

- Take calculated risks that propel your business forward while minimizing potential downsides
- Set clear, achievable goals and break them down into smaller milestones
- Negotiate effectively to achieve favorable outcomes
- Manage time efficiently to maximize productivity
- Communicate persuasively to influence others
- Adapt quickly to changing circumstances
- Build and maintain strong professional networks

As you'll see, being a successful entrepreneur is not about the money but the mindset.

So, are you ready to put in the work?

CHAPTER ONE

To Hell with "Normal"

The first property I ever bought was a giant, run-down building that sat on a 150,000-square-foot dumping ground. Sounds like a winner, right? The seller was a gravestone-manufacturing company that had gone bankrupt. Instead of throwing away their waste granite, they'd just dumped the giant stone pieces, along with tiles, concrete slabs, and garbage in general, onto the back of their property. Disadvantaged, distressed, and dirty, the place looked like a wasteland by the time I went to look at it. But I knew that in real estate, you can never take anything at face value.

I also knew that where you make your money isn't in the selling price of a property but in the purchasing price, and this one was way under market value. When I first started scouting properties, the traditional route of using websites such as Zillow, LoopNet, and Trulia wouldn't do. None of these platforms had the bargain prices I was looking for because their properties still had something going for them. I needed to find a property that no one wanted. So, I started attending court auctions for land and buildings that had gone into foreclosure.

Unfortunately, the courtroom was like a zoo, filled with a ton of other investors with the same idea. I knew that I hardly stood a chance against all these people.

So, I took an even bigger step back and asked, *What happens before a bankruptcy case goes to court?* I found a list of thousands of appraisers in Germany, where I lived at the time, who handled companies in trouble before they filed for bankruptcy. I found the right point people and emailed each one, asking if there were properties attached to their cases. The task was grueling; I was looking for a needle in a haystack. But the thing about looking for a needle in a haystack is that you only need to find one. Most of the appraisers never answered my inquiries. A couple of them acknowledged my inquiry but then never followed up about the property. And then, one day, someone replied.

The day I went to see the property, fifteen of us stood there, staring at the deconstructed mess. One by one, each of the other potential buyers walked away, shaking their heads and declaring the task of removing all the debris too expensive and too much work. They may as well have thrown tomatoes at the property. I, on the other hand, had a different reaction. I was beaming inside. I didn't understand why no one else was seeing what I saw. Yes, I'd need to do something with the debris, but why not take those stones and tiles and break them down into smaller pieces that could be used for the foundations of more office spaces and a parking garage? All we'd need was a little man power and a few excavating machines. This process would cost me peanuts compared to trying to haul the debris off the property.

Only one other buyer remained interested. He was from Switzerland, and he hadn't made it in person to actually see the property. Apparently, he, too, saw some potential there, and we entered into a small bidding war. Finally, after weeks of going back and forth, we agreed to stop driving the price up on each other and just meet at the notary on a set date. Whoever came in with the biggest offer would get the deal. That day, as luck would have it, the guy never showed up. (In hindsight, I now have a suspicion that he was hired by the seller just to drive the price up.) So, I bought the property for around $472,000. Ninety percent of the purchase was financed through hard lenders since banks didn't want to touch this property or me, a young foreign guy who'd never owned more than a car.

I was just twenty-six years old. Though I didn't know it at the time, that first deal laid the foundation, both literally and figuratively, for how I'd continue to conduct business and eventually build my empire. Every unconventional step of that deal and what happened next taught me lessons I learned quickly and now teach other entrepreneurs, including those outside the field of real estate. It was the groundwork that would make up every chapter in this book.

Back and Under: The Only Way Forward

What exactly is the contrarian way of doing business? It starts with a vision. Standing there in front of that heap of rubble, I didn't see what everyone else saw. Or, rather, I saw what no one else saw: potential. It's what I call "seeing backward." I'd already thought backward with the process of finding the property, rewinding to the point before a property price dropped. Now, I took the picture I wanted—a modern, bustling office building—and thought about the steps that would get that picture to become reality. Nobody could talk me out of that vision—not the other fourteen investors who walked away from it frowning, not the small town of seven thousand people who discarded the property and thought it was foolish to take on the mission to clean it up.

To outsiders, I seemed, at best, stupid and, at worst, insane. Here was this young, foreign guy who didn't know what he was getting himself into. What I was doing didn't make sense to them because I was focused on long-term goals they couldn't see, goals that went way beyond money or quick success. I was building the empire I'd dreamed of as a twelve-year-old kid living in Amsterdam, delivering newspapers before school (a story you'll hear more about later).

Like that first property, my whole life has been a field of giant boulders that seemed impossible to climb over. But instead of seeing these boulders as obstacles, I learned that to move them, I needed to look underneath the rocks for deeper understanding and hidden opportunities. I learned not to listen to the naysayers who declared something impossible. I learned that the only way to find rewards was to take calculated risks. And I wasn't alone. Take Elon Musk, for example. People thought he was nuts—until they watched him turn the car industry on its head and make space tourism an actual possibility.

> **I learned that the only way to find rewards was to take calculated risks.**

I didn't know it at the time, but I was following the same contrarian code that Musk and other greats had followed. Men and women such as Ray Kroc (McDonald's), Steve Jobs (Apple), and Sophia Amoruso (Nasty Gal), who challenged norms, ignored the critics, and built global empires. Even the ones who don't become industry titans still manage to forge their own paths to success, despite the naysayers. Think of that cousin who quit nursing school and started a kombucha company from her kitchen. Or your uncle who made a small fortune off his patented shoe-shining formula and retired early. These are all examples of entrepreneurs who swam against the current, ignored the critics, and took smart risks.

Nowadays, the term *entrepreneur* is overused. In 2025, an entrepreneur is hardly distinguishable from a freelancer. In fact, most entrepreneurs today have got their businesses down to a neat little system, making their work convenient and practical. They generate just enough growth each year to keep going and maybe take three weeks of vacation instead of two. Even though they may not technically have nine-to-five jobs, they still have a nine-to-five mindset. Their schedules might be more flexible, but their thinking is not. They're still operating from an invisible playbook that's been established by the corporate world with rules that are considered "normal" by most people.

This book is not for that kind of entrepreneur. It's for the kind that many people today would call the *contrarian entrepreneur*. The contrarian entrepreneur resembles the OG entrepreneur because they don't follow any rules. In fact, they don't even know what the so-called rules are. But they do have a code, which you'll learn more about soon.

When the World Stops, Keep Moving

There I was, with my first commercial real estate purchase. I was staring at a giant heap of rubble I'd just put every last penny I had into. And I was psyched. It was time to pull up my sleeves and get to work. The property was about a ninety-minute drive from my home in Munich. I'd wake up at 3:00 a.m. each morning to be there by 5:30 so I could open the gate for the construction crew and be present for any issue that might come up.

I had the perfect plan to finish the renovations before summer and then put the place back on the market. I even knew which companies I wanted to call to give first right of refusal. After borrowing another $210,000 to build office spaces, construct an apartment for the groundskeeper, and make everything shiny and new, the renovations were done. And then the unexpected happened, which no one could have been prepared for: the March 2020 pandemic lockdown. I'd just put all of my capital into a property that might sit there indefinitely.

I could easily have played the victim, and believe me, I felt like one at times. Instead, I decided to stay positive. I saw that this was a crisis that we were all having to face, not just me. I had three choices:

1. I could try to swim upstream and fight the current, but that seemed silly.
2. I could give up and just fall into the river, lose myself, and drown in the current; again, not an option.
3. I could wait on the banks of the river and hold on to what I could until the world restabilized.

My wife and I downsized. We moved into a smaller apartment and tried cutting our expenses in half while we buckled down and waited until the storm blew over. Meanwhile, I created a video viewing of the site for potential buyers so that once the lockdown ended, I'd be one step ahead of the game.

During that time, I thought about what I could be grateful for in the situation. At first, no bank would come near this deal, which is why I had to rely on hard lenders to cover 90 percent of the purchase. The rates were brutal, the timeline tighter than I liked, but I made it work. A few months in, once I'd cleaned up the numbers and the project looked less like a gamble and more like a plan, I managed to refinance. A local bank finally came on board—not for the purchase but for the renovation phase. I used the new loan to pay off the hard lenders and take control of the asset. So yes, by the time things got serious, I wasn't answering to the sharks anymore. Just the bank—and even they were starting to believe in the project. That was a huge relief since, during the pandemic, businesses all over the world were shutting down, allowing governments to bail them out of debt. In Germany, the government handed companies money like toilet paper, matching their total revenue from the previous year so that they could pay their employees, their rent, and all of their overhead expenses. All you had to do as a business owner was sign a contract as thick as the phone book.

My former business partner had had his best year yet the previous year, so he was handed a small fortune by the government. Believe me when I tell you that he went to town with that money. He bought himself a Ferrari, partied all the time, and traveled back and forth to Thailand several times. He seemed to be living the dream. But to me, free money is always a big red flag. If something feels too good to be true, it most likely is. And all the fine print that business owners signed off on without reading or understanding was going to become a landmine of regret.

No thanks, not for me, I thought. Instead, my company simply adapted to the lockdown. We did virtual meetings, measurements, and viewings. We still let people go to the construction sites to check out properties but, of course, had them keep their distance. For the most part, it was business as usual, albeit in unusual circumstances. Despite what everyone else around me was doing, I continued to work hard and simply adjusted my plans accordingly. A couple of years later, when the main government court in Berlin declared that the bailout money was never a gift, and that everyone, including my former partner, had to pay back that money, boy, was I glad I'd listened to my gut.

If It Doesn't Make Money, It Doesn't Make Sense

Soon, one of the fifteen buyers who had originally considered the building approached me about this new, cleaned-up version of it. He was interested in buying but then quickly balked at my asking price. You see, in Germany, people look down on the practice of flipping properties. Instead, property investors take a long-term approach to investments since the German government offers a tax-free perk for anyone who holds on to their property for at least ten years. I, personally, would rather fix and flip multiple properties and make a whole lot more than whatever amount of tax I might save down the road. But then, that's only one of many things I'd do differently as a contrarian.

This guy interested in buying my property didn't like this mindset. Resentful, he started to talk to other prospective buyers, spreading rumors that I had thrown all of the debris into a giant pit in the back of the building and then closed it off. The whole town jumped on the bandwagon and started campaigning against me to keep me from selling the property. I didn't know what to do. I had no way of proving he was wrong, and I had to rent or sell my property right away, or I'd be losing money by the minute.

Then a blessing came. It was disguised, as they often are, as yet another obstacle. I got a letter from the German government, which had been tipped off by one of the townspeople about my supposed violation of the law. The letter informed me that inspectors were going to do an excavation to see if the accusations were true. Oh yeah, and besides the pain in the neck that this was going to be, I also had to pay for it out of my own pocket. Twenty giant holes and a $38,000 bill later, the government, of course, found nothing.

The truth is, that nuisance actually did me a favor, because it cleared my name. When prospective renters and buyers came and asked me about the rumors, I could show them this government-issued certificate as official proof that I was not some unprincipled landowner. Because of my good reputation, I had secured loans from banks that had no business lending me money and signed deals with very few lawyers involved.

Many of my coaching clients say that becoming a millionaire is their number-one goal. In fact, about 90 percent of them openly admit that they would choose a million dollars over a solid reputation or brand. For me, my business isn't about the money but about my name. I can lose a million overnight, but my brand can always get me back my million and more. More than just insurance, though, my brand is ultimately the legacy I leave behind. For every transaction I conduct, I ask myself, "Is this the legacy I want to leave behind?"

> **I can lose a million overnight, but my brand can always get me back my million and more.**

Of course, money is one of the best parts of growing your empire. But if it's just money, then you'll have a problem with credibility. Elon Musk is not the richest person in the world because he only cares about money; he actually cares about changing something in the world. And because he already had that reputation, he was able to get investors to back him up when he bought Twitter (now X). Likewise, entrepreneurs Daniel Ek and Martin Lorentzon, founders of Spotify, still have a thriving product, even after Taylor Swift denounced them and pulled her music from the platform. Why? Because, despite one of the world's most successful musicians going against them, they had an enduring vision to support artists and curtail piracy efforts that, before long, even Swift couldn't argue against. Similarly, a true contrarian is concerned mostly with their long-term legacy.

Getting back to my story, about a month after COVID struck, I found a company that wanted to rent the property. Their only hesitation was that the location was inconvenient, since most of their employees lived about an hour's drive away. I couldn't let this deal slip through my fingers since I needed the gained capital to stay afloat. So, I got creative quickly. I offered to pay for all of the employees' fuel costs for the entire first year. After a few more rounds of negotiations, I finally had a tenant and could start replenishing my capital!

Four months after that, I got a call that someone else wanted to buy the building, and he wanted to do so in one week's time. The guy was German, and, like many of the potential buyers who'd walked away, he knew what I'd originally paid for the property less than a year before. But that didn't seem to bother him. His answer to these other investors was: "Why shouldn't he be charging that amount? It's a completely different piece of property now. You had the opportunity to flip the same property but didn't take it." The place sold for $1.7 million, at a cap rate of 7 percent. I had officially made my first million. Two years later, the buyer and I became business partners on another venture that's now thriving, which you'll read about later.

The Contrarian Advantage

A lot of people ask me, "Reza, why do you still buy office buildings? Haven't you heard that many people are working from home now?" That's exactly why now is the best time to buy those office buildings. I'm confident that remote work is just a phase that will pass in time. Why? Because leaders can't be made from Zoom calls and phone meetings. Home life has too many distractions that will keep people from forging ahead in their careers. You already see a lot of companies calling people back to the office because performance rates are low. Right now, I'm paying only a quarter or a third of the market rate. If I wait until the tides turn, it will be too late to get good prices on these buildings. So, I do what investment bankers on Wall Street do: I take profits on the way up and start dollar-cost averaging when the markets come down, which is when you regularly invest money into something, regardless of its price at the time. This approach lets you spread out your investment over time and hedge your bets.

Warren Buffett once said that it's wise for investors "to be fearful when others are greedy and to be greedy only when others are fearful."[1] As a contrarian, you will learn to think this way, too, so that you'll always stay a few steps ahead of the crowd.

> ### How to Spot a Contrarian in a Crowd
>
> - They deliberately think and act against popular trends and opinions.
> - They question what most people accept as true.
> - They push back against what others around them are saying.
> - They dare to explore paths that others are too afraid to even look at.
> - They live to disprove conventional wisdom.
> - They embrace failure because they do not see it as such.
> - They stay informed and always strive for more knowledge.
> - They seek out diverse perspectives.
> - They trust their own instincts.

---

1 Warren Buffett, "Berkshire Hathaway Inc. Shareholder Letter 1986," Berkshire Hathaway, February 27, 1987, https://www.berkshirehathaway.com/letters/1986.html.

CHAPTER TWO

Zero Is the New Million

Conventional thought: You need a lot of money to start a business.

Maverick truth: You can start from almost nothing.

Almost every young person I mentor thinks that to start a successful business, you need a lot of capital. They listen to their business school professors, the how-to books they devour, and the seasoned entrepreneurs they know who all followed a specific road map. These so-called experts will tell you to secure funding, find investors, or take out loans—essentially to gather as much financial backing as possible before you even think about launching your venture.

What if I told you that this is not only unnecessary but actually the totally wrong approach? The contrarian truth, which I have lived and continue to teach, is that success in business isn't about the amount of money you start with; it's about your creativity, determination, and strategic planning. Money isn't the be-all and end-all of entrepreneurship. In fact, starting with little to no capital can be the best thing you can do to build a solid foundation.

Take a moment to consider some of the most successful companies in the world today—Facebook, Ben & Jerry's, Hewlett-Packard, Spanx, Amazon, Cisco Systems, Virgin Group, Clif Bar, Disney, Nike, and Google. Each of these businesses started in humble settings—from garages to living rooms to home kitchens—with minimal financial resources. Their founders didn't let a lack of capital deter them. Instead, they focused on what they could do with the resources they had, leveraging their creativity and determination to build billion-dollar empires. They weren't so much concerned about making money as they were obsessed with making a change.

> **The contrarian truth, which I have lived and continue to teach, is that success in business isn't about the amount of money you start with; it's about your creativity, determination, and strategic planning.**

This chapter is dedicated to helping you understand how you can start a business with almost nothing. I'll show you how, with minimal resources, you can skip the line and start your business right now. You'll learn that setting yourself up to win is not about the money in your pocket but about the ingenuity in your mind and the fire in your belly.

Mind the Gap

In 2013, I moved from Dubai to a small city in Germany called Deggendorf. It's a quaint place in Bavaria, about 120 kilometers south of Munich, nestled in the picturesque Alps. Sounds like a mini-paradise, doesn't it? But the truth is, when I first got there, it was my own private hell. I was twenty years old, full of ambition and dreams, and was used to living with my mother and having a bustling social life in Dubai. Now, I found myself in a town where no one spoke English, and the residents were far from welcoming to outsiders.

Besides, I never planned on living in Germany. My original plan was to study in an English-speaking place. I had two tempting offers—one from a university in London and another from Canada. Both of these options, however, required a significant financial investment, not just for tuition but also for living expenses. I'd just sold my prized possession, my BMW 330—a car with a fierce engine, sleek design, and crazy pickup that made it addictive to drive. The idea of blowing the whole $20,000 I got from that sale on just one year of university, with no idea of how I'd pay for the other three years, was frightening. Germany, on the other hand, offered free education, and I had the option to live with my stepdad, who generously offered me free accommodations and the use of his car. This meant I could save the $20,000 and invest it in my future.

PRINCIPLE #1: IDENTIFY A SPECIFIC NEED

My decision to stay in Germany, although financially the smart thing to do, came with its challenges. Deggendorf, with a population of around thirty thousand people, had only a few spots for nightlife, which weren't particularly welcoming to foreigners, especially those who didn't speak German. As I tried to integrate into the local culture, I found myself feeling increasingly isolated. The language barrier, coupled with a noticeably racist vibe, made it difficult to connect with anyone my age. For the first time in my life, I was a true outsider.

As I struggled with these challenges, I also began to notice something important—an opportunity. The town was home to a university with a large international student population. I knew I must not be alone in feeling limited, since there were other foreign students at the university. Many of these students, like me, must have also found it difficult to socialize and integrate into the local community. They were being turned away from clubs and bars, not because of their behavior but because of their nationality and language. This exclusion was not only unfair but also left a significant portion of the student population without a place to chill, meet new people, and enjoy their time outside of class.

This realization sparked the idea that would eventually lead to my first business venture. I saw a clear need—an unmet demand for a social space where people like me could feel welcome. Other business owners in the town had overlooked this giant, gaping hole, probably because they were too focused on their own clientele or they simply didn't see the value in catering to a more diverse group. Whatever the reason, I was staring at this chasm, and the ideas started popping into my head. If you've ever used the Underground in London, you'll know that at nearly every station, a voice tells the passengers to "mind the gap between the train and the platform." That's exactly what I was doing: minding the gap between supply and demand.

At first, I thought about opening a shisha bar. Shisha, or hookah, is a popular social activity in the Middle East, and I knew from my time in Dubai that it could be a hit among students. However, finding the right location for a shisha bar proved challenging. I needed a space with good ventilation and also a pleasant ambiance—somewhere with windows and maybe an outdoor space. But all I could find were basement locations—dark, small, and completely wrong for the experience I wanted to create for customers.

PRINCIPLE #2: LEVERAGE CREATIVITY AND STRATEGY

It was during this search that I came across a large, empty venue that had once been a nightclub. The place was enormous—more than twenty thousand square feet—with a capacity for two thousand to three thousand people. It was a space that required a lot more than just a few hookah pipes and comfy seating. At first, I dismissed it as being far too big and too ambitious for my modest budget. But the more I thought about it, the more I realized that it could be exactly what I was looking for—if I looked at it the right way.

I reached out to the previous owners to find out why the nightclub had failed. Their reasons were revealing—they had struggled to attract a steady stream of patrons, largely because they didn't have the right connections with the local university or the student body. Instead, they had focused on the local population, which was small and already loyal to the existing clubs in the area.

A light bulb went off in my head. The previous owners had tried to compete with the other local clubs on their turf—that was the source of their failure. But I wasn't interested in competing for the same customers. Instead, I saw an opportunity to create something new, something that filled the gap no one else was seeing. What they saw as an obstacle—the town's insular thinking—I saw as an opportunity. This is how a contrarian thinks.

As an entrepreneur, you need to look for the gaps in the market, the unmet needs, and the problems that others have overlooked or dismissed. These are the areas where you can make a real impact, often with far less money than you might think. Take, for example, mobile farmers markets in cities around the world where fresh produce is scarce. Or pop-up repair shops and fix-it clinics where anything from small appliances to clothing can be rehabilitated instead of thrown away in an effort to discourage waste.

Connection over Cash

PRINCIPLE #3: BUILD STRATEGIC ALLIANCES

My nightclub was meant to solve a problem too—namely, international students who wanted a comfortable, cool place to socialize. I knew that if I could make this work, it could be something special. The challenge was how to pull it off with just $20,000 and zero experience.

One of the most critical steps I took was forming a partnership with a local entrepreneur who already had experience in the nightclub industry. He was well known in the area for his successful bars, and he had the industry knowledge and connections I seriously lacked. We decided to open the club as a fifty-fifty partnership. My partner would bring his expertise, and I would bring the vision and the hard work. The honeymoon period didn't last past the first week. My partner was a busy man, with multiple businesses to run, and he didn't have the same level of emotional investment in the club as I did. This meant that a lot of the day-to-day responsibilities fell on my shoulders. I found myself taking on tasks I had never imagined—painting the walls, laying flooring, setting up the bar, and managing the staff.

This partnership was crucial for several reasons. First, it allowed us to share the financial burden. The initial investment to get the club up and running was around $35,000, and by splitting the costs, we both reduced our financial risk. Still, we needed more to open a club that size. We closed sponsorship deals with Coca-Cola and vodka and beer companies; we would only sell their brands of beverages in exchange for up-front royalties. This exchange got us another $35,000. This was important because it meant that I didn't have to stretch every last dollar even further to cover all the expenses. Second, I now had access to my partner's network. He had connections with suppliers, local authorities, and other business owners I simply didn't have. This network was invaluable in running a nightclub, from securing permits to sourcing supplies at the best prices.

I needed to maximize the impact of every dollar I spent. Traditional marketing methods were out of the question—I simply didn't have the budget for big campaigns or flashy promotions. Instead, I had to get creative and think about how I could leverage what I did have to create buzz and draw students in. In Deggendorf, most of the local clubs only operated on Fridays and Saturdays. During the week, students had nowhere to go. I decided to introduce a new concept: a midweek event specifically for them called Halftime. The idea was simple but effective: On Wednesdays, everything—drinks, entry fees, and even snacks—was half price. Students loved it, of course.

PRINCIPLE #4: INVEST IN YOUR CUSTOMER'S EXPERIENCE

But I didn't stop there. I knew that just offering discounts wasn't enough—I needed to create a unique spin on the whole club experience to keep students coming back week after week. I reached out to a local energy drink company and proposed a partnership. In exchange for sponsorship, they provided us with free drinks that we could distribute during our events. This not only reduced our costs but also gave us a cool, youthful brand to associate with the club. It was a win-win.

We set up promotional tents on campus, handed out flyers throughout the whole city every week, and specifically targeted student apartment buildings. We even branded coffee cups with the nightclub's logo. I named the club Barcode to connect with the tech-savvy vibe of the young population, since barcodes are everywhere in our daily lives. To me, the concept symbolized quick access and instant connection, and I wanted to bring that into the club. We tied everything back to this theme, from the barcode-style entry passes to drink vouchers that could be scanned for discounts or special offers. The club's design was sleek and simple, reflecting this high-tech theme. Barcode wasn't just a name; it became an identity that resonated with students, making the club feel like an extension of their digital lifestyle. We wanted customers to feel like part of something special, something that was just for them.

The response was insane. At our first Halftime event, we had more than seven hundred students lining up to get in. Do you have any idea what seven hundred students look like on a quiet street in Bavaria? They were like a giant, noisy mob. Inside, the club was packed and the atmosphere was electric, and word spread quickly. Students started talking about the club on social media, sharing pictures and videos of the events and spreading a serious case of FOMO to anyone who hadn't been yet.

By focusing on the student market, offering discounts, and creating a unique experience, we were able to fill the club every week without spending a fortune on advertising. This is a crucial lesson for any entrepreneur—when resources are limited, creativity becomes your most valuable asset. Look for ways to stretch your budget, partner with other brands or businesses, and create a unique value proposition that sets you apart from the competition.

As the nightclub began to gain traction, some of the existing club owners in town tried to emulate Barcode's strategies, offering similar discounts or themed nights, but they couldn't catch up. That's because Barcode's success was rooted in something deeper than just clever marketing—it was about understanding and valuing our customers in a way that the other clubs never had. For them, it was a case of too little, too late.

When "No Gain" Is Worth the Pain

PRINCIPLE #5: SACRIFICE PERSONAL GAIN FOR YOUR BUSINESS'S GROWTH

As the club started to get more popular, I faced a new challenge: how to financially sustain its long-term success. The natural inclination when a business starts making money is to start paying yourself, especially if, like me, you've been working without pay for months. But I knew that if I wanted the club to succeed, I had to reinvest every penny back into the business. So for the first two years, I didn't take a salary. Every dollar we earned went back into the club. We upgraded the sound system, improved the lighting, invested in better decor, and organized bigger and better events.

It wasn't easy—there were times when I struggled to cover my personal expenses, and the temptation to take some money out of the business was strong, especially when I saw my partner living a luxurious lifestyle with the money he made from his other businesses. But it was totally worth it. The improvements we made helped attract more customers, not just from the local student population but also from neighboring towns.

PRINCIPLE #6: INSPIRE LOYALTY AND COMMITMENT

But I knew I couldn't be the only one invested in the club. And I'd seen that, even though he was financially invested, my partner wasn't emotionally present. I needed to build a team that wanted to see the club succeed as much as I did, beyond the dollar bill. This meant creating an environment where my team would feel valued, appreciated, and concerned about the club's success. One of the ways I did this was by involving my employees in the decision-making process. I didn't just give orders and expect them to follow—I asked for their input, listened to their ideas, and made them feel as if they were part of something bigger.

When we planned events, I'd gather the team together to brainstorm ideas and discuss how we could make each event a success. I also made sure to recognize and reward hard work. When someone went above and beyond, I acknowledged it, whether it was a simple *thank you* or by giving them more responsibility. In a matter of weeks, everyone working at the club became more than just employees—they became partners in the club's success. They took pride in their work, went the extra mile to get things running smoothly, and were willing to step up when we needed extra help with something. Building that team was far more important than any financial investment.

PRINCIPLE #7: DON'T AVOID RISK—CALCULATE IT

One of the most challenging aspects of starting a business with limited capital is managing risk. When you don't have a lot of money to fall back on, every decision carries more weight. This is where calculated risk-taking comes into play.

In Barcode's early days, I had to make many difficult decisions that involved balancing risk and reward. One of the biggest decisions was where to allocate our limited funds. I knew that we needed to invest in the club's infrastructure—upgrading the sound system, improving the lighting, and making the space more inviting—but I also knew that these investments carried significant risks. If the club didn't succeed, I would have nothing to show for the money I had spent.

To manage these risks, I took a calculated approach. Instead of spending all our money up front, I made incremental investments, testing each one to see how it impacted the club's success. For example, we started with a modest sound system and gradually upgraded it as the club gained popularity. This allowed us to spread out the financial burden and minimize the risk of overcommitting our resources.

Another key aspect of risk management is learning to adapt quickly. In the early days, we tried opening the club on Saturdays in addition to our Wednesday student Halftime nights. But that idea ended up bombing—many students went home for the weekend, and the local population was still loyal to the established clubs. For me to even switch on the lights cost $700. That plus paying my employees to come in was like robbing myself from my own pockets. So I decided to stay closed on Saturdays, which theoretically should have been my best night.

This kind of pivoting and changing course is crucial to managing the risks associated with running a nightclub, or any business, for that matter. As you'll see later, it certainly applies to real estate. By being able to pivot, we were able to conserve our resources and focus on the areas where we were most likely to succeed.

> **Starting with almost nothing has instilled in me a deep sense of determination and resilience.**

PRINCIPLE #8: STAY HUNGRY

Here's where the biggest advantage lies in starting your business with almost nothing: You hunger for success. No trust fund child or heir to wealth will ever know the fire in your belly I talked about earlier. They'll never feel as a kid, the way I did, that urge to shoulder their own weight and not be a burden to anyone else. And they'll never know the satisfaction that comes when you look around yourself and see the magic you helped create by turning nothing into something incredible.

> **Hunger is a powerful motivator. When you're hungry for success, you're willing to do whatever it takes to achieve your goals.**

Throughout my long and winding journey, one thing has remained constant: my hunger for success. This hunger has been the driving force behind everything I've done, from selling my car to starting the nightclub to working long hours without pay to ensure success. It's what has kept me going through the challenges and setbacks and what continues to motivate me to this day. Starting with almost nothing has instilled in me a deep sense of determination and resilience. When you don't have a financial safety net, failure is not an option. This lack creates a sense of urgency and a drive to succeed that is hard to replicate when you have the luxury of financial security. It pushes you to work harder, think more creatively, and take risks others might shy away from.

But this hunger isn't just about financial success—it's also about the desire to build something meaningful, something that lasts. I've always had big dreams, and I've never been afraid to pursue them, even when the odds were against me. This drive has been the key to my success, and it's something that I believe every entrepreneur needs to cultivate. Hunger is a powerful motivator. When you're hungry for success, you're willing to do whatever it takes to achieve your goals. You're not afraid of hard work, and you're not discouraged by setbacks. Instead, you see every challenge as an opportunity to learn and grow. This hunger is what will drive you to keep going, even when the road gets tough.

> **The contrarian truth is that you don't need a lot of money to start your business. What you need are a clear vision, the determination to see it through, and the willingness to do whatever it takes to make it happen.**

The contrarian truth is that you don't need a lot of money to start your business. What you need are a clear vision, the determination to see it through, and the willingness to do whatever it takes to make it happen. If you can do that, you can start from zero and build something extraordinary. The most important resources you have are not in your bank account—they're in your mind, your heart, and your spirit. Harness these, and you can turn zero into a million anytime, anywhere.

In this chapter, you've seen how sacrificing short-term gains for long-term growth and maintaining a relentless hunger for success can make all the difference. Now let's explore what to do when your million-dollar plan takes a wrong turn.

> **The most important resources you have are not in your bank account—they're in your mind, your heart, and your spirit.**

Maverick Takeaways

- You don't need a fortune to begin—start with what you have and scale strategically.

- Collaboration can help you reach new heights, especially when you lack financial resources.

- When money is tight, innovation is your greatest asset. Think outside the box to stretch your budget.

- Reinvest your early earnings back into the business—delay personal gain for long-term success.

- The desire to prove yourself and build something meaningful will push you further than any financial safety net ever could.

- Be prepared to adapt quickly when something isn't working. Smart, calculated risks lead to sustainable growth.

CHAPTER THREE

Expect the Unexpected

Conventional thought: You need a perfect business plan.

Maverick truth: Plans change, so be flexible.

Pivot or Bust

In July 2019, I made one of the biggest decisions of my life—I bought my first piece of real estate. I had everything planned out perfectly. The property was set to go back on the market the following summer, and I was confident it would be a profitable sale. Every detail was accounted for, from the renovations to the marketing strategy, and I was sure I'd covered all my bases. The plan was simple: purchase, improve, and sell for a substantial profit. It was a formula that had worked for countless investors before me, and I saw no reason why it wouldn't work for me, too.

But as March 2020 rolled around, the global pandemic kicked all of us on our butts. Overnight, the world went into lockdown, and my perfect plan was thrown out the window. Borders closed, economies slowed, and the real estate market, which had seemed so promising, became a minefield of risks. Suddenly, everything I had anticipated changed, and my carefully laid plans were no longer viable.

In the blink of an eye, I found myself in uncharted territory. The strategies I had been so confident about were now obsolete. Buyers vanished, financing became uncertain, and the idea of making a quick sale evaporated into thin air. I'd already been down that road, losing many nights of sleep when things went awry with the nightclub. I saw that worrying over the unexpected didn't stop the unexpected from happening. And going down that road got me nowhere. This time around, instead of panicking, I chose a better path.

I adapted. I shifted my focus, explored alternative ways to utilize the property, and navigated the challenges that came with this new reality. Flexibility became my most valuable asset, and it's what saved my business during one of the most unpredictable times in modern history. I'd already learned to think outside the box. But now, there was no box. I had to supercharge my creativity engines and come up with methods I'd never consider under normal circumstances. I explored rental options, partnerships, and even longer-term holds that I'd previously dismissed. It wasn't easy, and it wasn't what I had planned for, but it was necessary. As the saying goes, desperate times call for desperate measures.

This chapter is about expecting the unexpected. If you're used to clinging to a perfect business plan, you're setting yourself up to lose. The reality is, no matter how well you plan, something will always go wrong. And when it does, your ability to pivot on a dime will determine whether you sink or swim.

As I learned quickly, life doesn't care about your plans. Markets crash, pandemics happen, competitors change tactics, and consumer behavior shifts. The most successful businesspeople are those who can adapt to these changes, who can get to a roadblock and adjust their strategies accordingly. This is not just a skill; it's a mindset, a way of thinking that embraces uncertainty and sees it as an opportunity rather than a threat.

Most business advice you'll hear revolves around the need for a perfect, airtight business plan. Consultants and professors will tell you that without one, you're just wandering aimlessly, doomed to fail. Conventional thought says that if you plan everything to the last detail and execute that plan flawlessly, then you'll achieve success. The business world is full of books, seminars, and consultants who emphasize the importance of detailed planning, and for good reason. It helps you identify your goals, allocate resources, and anticipate challenges. But that's where the value ends.

Here's the contrarian truth: Plans change. Life doesn't care about your perfect plan. The market doesn't care, customers don't care, vendors don't care—you get the point. The people who thrive in this unpredictable world are the ones who know how to adapt when everything falls apart. These people know that a perfect plan doesn't work in an imperfect world. My real estate story is just one example. I had a solid plan, but the pandemic forced me to rethink everything.

Having to pivot is part of the success story of almost every business out there. Consider the example of Blockbuster. They had a perfect plan—or so they thought. They dominated the video rental market and were perfectly positioned to continue that dominance into the new millennium. But then Netflix came along, offering a new way to rent movies by mail and, later, through streaming. Blockbuster had the opportunity to buy Netflix for a fraction of what it's worth today, but they passed on it, sticking rigidly to their business plan. We all know how that story ended. Blockbuster is now a cautionary tale, a reminder that no matter how successful your business is, if you're not willing to adapt, you're destined for failure.

> **Your ability to pivot, adapt to new circumstances, and adjust your strategy in response to real-world feedback is what will ultimately determine your success.**

On the other hand, Netflix, the disruptor, demonstrated incredible flexibility. They started as a DVD rental service and then pivoted to streaming as technology evolved. Today, Netflix is a global entertainment powerhouse, not because they had a perfect plan from the start, but because they were willing to change their plan when the world changed around them. Netflix understood that the future of media consumption was moving online, and they were quick to shift their focus. They invested heavily in content creation, technology, and global expansion, all while their competitors were still clinging to outdated models.

The lesson here is clear: In business, flexibility is not just an asset; it's a necessity. Your ability to pivot, adapt to new circumstances, and adjust your strategy in response to real-world feedback is what will ultimately determine your success. Flexibility allows you to stay ahead of the curve, anticipate changes in the market, and capitalize on opportunities that others might miss.

Being flexible means building adaptability into your plans and preparing for the unexpected. It's about knowing where you want to go but being willing to take different paths to get there.

> **Being flexible means building adaptability into your plans and preparing for the unexpected. It's about knowing where you want to go but being willing to take different paths to get there.**

Planning: A Reality Check

When I bought that property back in 2019, I had no idea that a global pandemic was on the horizon. My plan, as perfect as it seemed, was suddenly obsolete. I could have sat back and blamed some virus or the government for ruining my business, but instead, I asked myself a different question: "How can I adapt to this new reality?" This is the mindset you need to cultivate if you want to succeed in the long term. It's not about having a perfect plan; it's about having the right mindset.

Your business plan should never be set in stone. It should be a living, breathing ideology that can pivot its practicals at a moment's notice. The goal is to create a flexible one that can survive the unexpected challenges that will inevitably come your way. In the television show *Suits*, Harvey Specter, one of the main characters, embodies this principle perfectly. Harvey is a suave, top lawyer who's known for never losing. But his secret isn't that he has a perfect plan for every case. Harvey understands that in the courtroom—as in business—things rarely go as planned. In one memorable scene, he explains that he avoids going to trial because trials are unpredictable, and once you're in front of a jury, anything can happen. That's why he prefers to negotiate settlements: It keeps him in control, where outcomes are shaped by strategy, not chance.

One of the most common mistakes I see in the business world is an overreliance on planning. Entrepreneurs can become so attached to their original plans that they fail to see when those plans are no longer viable. They cling to their strategies, hoping that if they just stick with them long enough, things will work out. But in reality, this kind of rigidity often leads to failure. The most successful entrepreneurs are those who can detach themselves from their plans, look at the situation objectively, and then make the necessary changes.

> **Your business plan should never be set in stone. It should be a living, breathing ideology that can pivot its practicals at a moment's notice.**

Unleash the Power Plays

In business, there are certain moves that give you an edge, like the high-risk, high-reward decisions that can make or break your success. I call these Power Plays—because when you master them, you'll be able to dominate the game. If you're serious about breaking the rules and succeeding where others fail, these Power Plays will keep you ahead of the curve.

POWER PLAY #1: MASTER EMOTIONAL CONTROL

In business, problems are constant. But it's not the problems that matter—it's how you solve them, with a balance between emotion and logic. You need to harness the raw energy of emotion without letting it cloud your judgment. Passion and intensity are what push you forward, but if you don't control them, you'll end up making reckless decisions. That's where logic steps in. Logic keeps your mind sharp, focused, and strategic. It allows you to step back, assess situations calmly, and act based on facts, not impulse. Imagine a crisis hits—your gut reaction is to panic. But real power comes from controlling that emotion and asking yourself, "What are the facts? What's the smartest move?"

POWER PLAY #2: SET RELENTLESS TARGETS

> **Every move you make should bring you closer to your target.**

If you're building an empire, your goals need to be relentless. Without them, you'll be flailing, wasting time on battles that don't matter. Every move you make should bring you closer to your target. During the pandemic, my goal was crystal clear: survive and adapt. That clarity dictated every decision I made, and it's why I came out stronger. Don't just set vague goals such as "I want to be successful." Be specific. Say, "I want to hit $1 million in revenue" or "I want to dominate a new market in the next year." When your goals are sharp, you know exactly when to fight and when to walk away.

> **When your goals are sharp, you know exactly when to fight and when to walk away.**

POWER PLAY #3: KILL WHAT'S NOT WORKING

The biggest mistake you can make is sticking to something just because you've put time, money, or effort into it. In business, this is called the sunk cost fallacy, and it's a trap. A real hustler knows when to kill what's not working. Think of it like a bear with its paw stuck in a tree trunk, reaching for honey. He's getting stung by bees, but he won't let go because he's already holding the honeycomb. Smart entrepreneurs are the ones who know when to let go before this happens.

> **The biggest mistake you can make is sticking to something just because you've put time, money, or effort into it.**

POWER PLAY #4: PIVOT LIKE A SHARK

In business, being able to pivot on a dime is what separates the elite from the average. If your strategy isn't working, change it. If your product isn't selling, shift your market. I've had to pivot many times in my career—whether it was changing my target market or adjusting my product line. When one path didn't lead to success, I didn't stubbornly keep walking it—I found a better way.

POWER PLAY #5: BE A SAVAGE LEARNER

Flexibility requires you to stay sharp. To dominate, you need to be more informed than everyone around you. That means you have to be a savage learner, always seeking out new information, studying the competition, and knowing the trends before they hit. In business, knowledge is power—but only if you hunt for it.

Take my third real estate deal. The property was a ten-thousand-square-foot space with a gym that had gone bankrupt during the pandemic. The deal was shaky, but I didn't give up. I dug deep, did my homework, and tracked down the gym's owner. Turns out, they had found a new investor and were back on their feet. Armed with that knowledge, I was able to turn a bad deal into a win. (I'll tell you more about this deal later in the book.)

**In business, knowledge is power—
but only if you hunt for it.**

POWER PLAY #6: BUILD AN UNBREAKABLE MINDSET

At the end of the day, flexibility starts with your mindset. If you want to rule the game, you need to be mentally unbreakable. Every setback is just a lesson, every failure a stepping stone. Being adaptable means you're ready to rise, no matter what. When things get tough, the weak fold. But you? You keep pushing forward.

Four Essential Face-Offs for a Flexible Business Model

Success in business starts with mastering the internal sparring matches that happen in your head every day. These mini-battles between conflicting forces—will versus skill, mission versus plan—determine how well you adapt and thrive.

Here are the four key face-offs to help you sharpen your thinking and keep your business agile.

ENEMIES VERSUS COMPETITORS

Emotionally, it's easy to view everyone as an enemy, but this mindset is a trap. Competitors are not enemies; they're entities with strategies and weaknesses, just like you. An enemy might have hidden threats, requiring careful observation and strategic planning. Learning to differentiate between the two allows you to approach them accordingly.

In one of my earliest real estate ventures, I attended an auction with several other bidders. At the time, I saw everyone in the room as an enemy, someone who was out to take what I wanted. This mindset clouded my judgment and made me anxious. But as I gained more experience, I realized that most of these people weren't out to get me personally; they were just trying to do business, the same as me. By shifting my mindset, I was able to approach these situations more calmly and strategically.

In another scenario, I found myself competing against a larger company for a prime piece of real estate. Initially, I viewed them as an enemy, a massive force that I couldn't possibly overcome. But as I analyzed the situation, I realized that they had weaknesses—specifically, their size made them slow to act. By being nimbler and more responsive, I was able to secure the property before they could. This experience taught me the importance of seeing competitors for what they are: rivals who can be outmaneuvered, not enemies who must be destroyed.

WILL VERSUS SKILL

Your will to succeed is important, but it's your skills that matter more. Will alone won't make you successful. Investing in your skills—whether it's learning new technologies, mastering market analysis, or understanding industry cycles—will carry you through when the going gets tough.

> **Will alone won't make you successful.**

For example, when I first entered the real estate market, I had a strong will to succeed, but I quickly realized that willpower alone wasn't enough. I needed to develop my skills—understanding market trends, negotiating deals, and managing properties. These skills didn't come overnight; they took time and effort to develop. But they're what allowed me to navigate the challenges I faced and ultimately succeed in the industry.

It's the same for any business. You can have all the will in the world, but if you don't have the skills to back it up, you're going to struggle. This is why continuous learning and skill development are so important. The more skilled you are, the more flexible you can be, because you'll have the tools you need to adapt to different situations.

One of the most valuable skills I've developed is the ability to analyze market data. This skill has allowed me to make informed decisions about when to buy, sell, or hold properties, even in uncertain times. While willpower is essential for driving you forward, it's your skills that determine whether you succeed or fail.

> **You can have all the will in the world, but if you don't have the skills to back it up, you're going to struggle.**

MISSION VERSUS PLAN

Your mission is your long-term vision, but your plan is how you achieve it. The mission might be to build a real estate empire, but the plan will change depending on the circumstances. For example, my mission in real estate has always been to build a diverse and profitable portfolio. But the way I've gone about that has changed over time. When the market was booming, my plan was to buy and sell properties quickly. But when the market slowed down, I had to pivot to a buy-and-hold strategy, focusing on generating rental income rather than quick sales.

> **Your mission is your long-term vision, but your plan is how you achieve it.**

It helps to remember that your plan is just a tool to help you achieve your mission. If the tool isn't working, it's time to find a new one. This might mean changing your business model, entering a new market, or even rethinking your product or service offerings. The key is to stay focused on the mission but be willing to change the plan as needed.

DREAM VERSUS REALITY

Dreaming big is important, but you also need to stay grounded in reality. Your dreams should inspire you, but your actions should be based on the current circumstances. Don't let your dreams cloud your judgment. For instance, when I first started in real estate, I had a dream of building a massive portfolio in a short amount of time. But the reality was that the market was more competitive than I had anticipated, and financing was harder to secure. I had to adjust my expectations and my strategy, focusing on smaller, more achievable goals. This didn't mean I gave up on my dream; it meant I adapted to the reality of the situation.

It's crucial to strike a balance between dreaming big and staying grounded. Your dreams should push you forward, but your actions need to be based on reality. This means constantly reassessing the situation, staying informed about market trends, and being willing to adjust your strategy when necessary.

Patience Is Power: The Art of Letting Go

It's funny how life throws curveballs at you when you least expect them, forcing you to adapt in ways you never thought possible. For me, this lesson came two years ago, in the form of a government raid.

My wife and I were supposed to drive from Munich to Holland for an embassy appointment, and I decided to drive there the night before instead, thinking I could sleep in the car for a few hours along the way. At around 5:00 a.m., just as I was about to rest near the Holland border, I got a call from a police officer, who told me there was a squad standing in front of my house in Munich, armed with a court order to enter my home.

Apparently, I was under suspicion of tax evasion. It hit me like a ton of bricks. My home, my office, my CPA's office—all were being raided and seized simultaneously. I was terrified. I felt helpless, like I had lost control over everything I'd built. To be honest, I thought about giving up. At that moment, all I could think about was my dream going up in smoke.

What followed was six months of waiting—six months of not knowing whether I'd go to jail and lose everything. My accounts were frozen, my documents confiscated. Even simple things like paying for gas became impossible without help. It was a disaster in every sense of the word. I couldn't sleep at night because every knock on the door felt like it could be the police coming to take me away.

Yet, amid all this chaos, one unexpected ally came to my rescue: patience. My lawyer's advice was simple: Do nothing. Don't react, don't panic, don't try to fix things immediately. "We'll deal with this in court," he told me. "There's no reason to fight it now." At first, it sounded insane—how could I just sit there and do nothing when everything was on the line? Is this what Harvey from *Suits* would do? But in hindsight, it was exactly what I needed to hear.

As the investigation dragged on, I had to make a decision: either put my entire life on hold or keep moving forward and let the universe do its thing. I chose to keep going. While business associates thought I should lie low, I closed not one but two new deals.

The key was to let go. When something isn't working—whether it's a tenant dragging their feet on signing a lease or a business deal that's not closing—overthinking becomes your biggest enemy. Today, I no longer push for results when things aren't falling into place. I present my strongest case, then I let go. I trust that the right outcomes will follow if I've done my part. Patience has taught me to let time work in my favor, and that lesson has been invaluable in my journey.

> **When something isn't working—whether it's a tenant dragging their feet on signing a lease or a business deal that's not closing—overthinking becomes your biggest enemy.**

Two years later, after countless sleepless nights and uncertainty, the investigation concluded with the realization that the accusations were baseless. It turned out to be a mistake, and all charges were dropped.

When the Door Doesn't Open, Knock on a Different One

When I was living in Munich, I realized something important: The environment was choking my growth. The real estate market was tight-knit, and as a young Middle Eastern entrepreneur, breaking into the local network was like banging my head against a wall. After a decade of hustling and still not getting the high ROI I wanted on all my hard work, I made a game-changing decision—I moved. That move transformed everything. Within a year, I established connections I couldn't get after ten years in Munich.

> **Flexibility is knowing when to shift not just your tactics but your entire environment.**

Moving wasn't easy; I had finally started to feel I had roots in Munich. Yet I knew the local market wasn't giving me what I needed. That choice opened doors I'd been knocking on for years. It taught me that flexibility is knowing when to shift not just your tactics but your entire environment. Don't get too comfortable where you are. Whether it's a new city, a new market, or even a new business model, sometimes the best way forward is stepping away from what's familiar and pursuing opportunities somewhere else.

> **Don't get too comfortable where you are. Whether it's a new city, a new market, or even a new business model, sometimes the best way forward is stepping away from what's familiar and pursuing opportunities somewhere else.**

As you move forward, remember this: It's not the perfect plan that gets you where you want to go—it's your ability to throw that plan out the window when it stops working. Flexibility is your edge. Cultivate the mindset that welcomes change and always be prepared to roll with the punches.

Whether you're staring down a pandemic, an economic shift, or a personal setback, your ability to adapt is going to determine whether you make it or not. Let go of outdated ideas, embrace new strategies, and own the uncertainty that comes with being a true entrepreneur. The path to success can be forged only by you, one bold, adaptable move at a time. So, keep it flexible, stay sharp, and always be ready to expect the unexpected. That's how you don't give up until you win.

It's not the perfect plan that gets you where you want to go—it's your ability to throw that plan out the window when it stops working.

Maverick Takeaways

- No plan is ever perfect. Flexibility in your business model is the key to survival when the unexpected hits.
- Embrace chaos as opportunity. When plans fall apart, see it as a chance to pivot and discover new paths.
- The market doesn't care about your plan. It's your ability to adapt that defines success, not your ability to stick to the script.
- Let go of sunk costs. Be willing to abandon what's not working, even if you've invested heavily—pivoting is a power move.
- Stay open to learning. Flexibility is fueled by constant learning and the willingness to adjust strategies based on real-world feedback.
- Build plans with room for change. The best plans aren't rigid; they allow for quick adjustments and creative solutions when things go sideways.

CHAPTER FOUR

Nurture Rules Nature

Conventional thought:
Entrepreneurs are born, not made.

Maverick truth:
Entrepreneurship is a decision.

The Grunt Work That Built Me

People often assume that successful entrepreneurs are somehow destined for greatness, as if it's in their DNA. But entrepreneurship isn't a birthright. Success comes down to the choices you make every day—how you handle setbacks, how you push forward, and how you take control of your future. Entrepreneurs are not a special breed; they are people who decided to take action and significant risks.

Donald Trump, being born into a wealthy family, faced the choice of either building on his father's legacy or finding his own path. He chose to work hard, expanding his father's real estate empire and taking bold risks that would define his career. Contrast that with his older brother, Fred Trump Jr., who chose a different path. Despite being the eldest son and initially expected to follow in his father's footsteps, Fred struggled with alcoholism and ultimately passed away at a young age. His story serves as a reminder that success is not determined by where you start. Both brothers shared the same DNA. They had access to the same resources and opportunities, yet the outcomes of their lives were vastly different.

> **Entrepreneurs are not a special breed; they are people who decided to take action and significant risks.**

When I started out, I wasn't sitting in a cushy office, getting spoon-fed opportunities by wealthy connections. No one handed me anything. I had to grind from the very bottom, working jobs that most people wouldn't consider applying for. I took whatever work I could get, and I mean *anything*: cleaning offices, delivering newspapers, scrubbing toilets, and working the front desk at a gym. Those were jobs I needed just to survive, not because I had some grand plan to become an entrepreneur. But every single one of those jobs built the foundation for my future.

One of the hardest jobs I had was working at Burger King in Schiphol Airport, in Amsterdam. Schiphol is one of Europe's busiest hubs, with around fifteen hundred flights landing and taking off every single day. It felt like every one of those passengers stopped by for a Whopper and fries on my shift. I ran the busiest station in that Burger King, doing the work of three people. Between the scorching heat from the deep fryer stinging my skin and the never-ending line of starving travelers, I felt like a one-man sweatshop. And there was no extra help—just me, grinding away.

Why did I keep working there? I thought if I worked hard enough, someone would notice. Maybe my manager would see how much effort

I was putting in, and I would get a raise. Maybe they would recognize my potential and give me more responsibility. But here is what happened when I finally asked for that raise: *nothing*. The answer was a cold, hard no. No discussion. No appreciation for the extra effort. Just no.

That was the moment it hit me: No one will value your time the way you do. You can work yourself into the ground, but if you are doing it for someone else, you are still building their dream, not your own. They were making money off my hard work, and all I got in return was a paycheck that barely covered my bills.

That job taught me how the world really works. You can be the hardest worker in the room, but if you are working for someone else, you are just a cog in their machine. And here is the harsh reality: That machine will keep running with or without you. In my case, that deep fryer would keep making fries whether I was there or not. That was the moment I realized I did not want to be a cog anymore. I wanted to build my own machine.

Every job I've had has taught me a lesson in what I *did not* want. I did not want to be stuck in a system that did not recognize my value. I did not want to spend my life working toward someone else's goals. But those jobs also taught me something crucial: They taught me how to spot inefficiencies. They showed me how businesses run and how character is built from the ground up, one brick at a time.

Wherever you are working right now, take the time to study your environment. Look for cracks in the system. It could be the way your team communicates (or doesn't), how your company manages its time, or even how customers are treated. Observe how things are done and make mental notes on what could be done better. This habit will help you not only improve your current performance but also build the skill set you need to run your own business in the future. Every problem you identify and fix makes you a better entrepreneur.

> **I realized that if I wanted my ideas to come to life, I had to be in control. I had to be the one calling the shots.**

For example, when I lived in Dubai, I worked at a gym. Every day, I stood at the front desk, manually buzzing people in one by one. It was an inefficient process that wasted time for both me and the customers. I suggested to the manager that we install an automated entry system. With a key card, members could walk right in, and I could focus on selling memberships or helping with workouts—doing something more valuable than just buzzing people through the door. My boss dismissed the idea as if it was irrelevant, like I did not know what I was talking about. He didn't see the inefficiency I saw. But here's the kicker: Fifteen years later, almost every gym in the world uses that exact system. That was a wake-up call for me. I realized that if I wanted my ideas to come to life, I had to be in control. I had to be the one calling the shots.

When you spot inefficiencies or come up with innovative ideas, own them. If your current boss doesn't listen—fine. But don't let that stop you from thinking like an entrepreneur. Write down those ideas, keep track of them, and when you have the chance to build something for yourself, implement them. Taking control of your ideas now will prepare you to lead effectively when you're the one running the show.

Wherever you work, train yourself to look beyond the surface. Is the customer experience smooth, or are there consistent pain points? Are resources being wasted? Observe how teams communicate and how time is managed. Once you start noticing these cracks, you'll realize how many opportunities are hidden in plain sight. It's not just about doing your job—it's about thinking like an owner, not an employee.

> **Taking control of your ideas now will prepare you to lead effectively when you're the one running the show.**

Turning Point: A Promise to Change My Life

There was a defining moment—a single point in time that made me realize I could not keep working the way I was. I was eighteen years old, living in Dubai with my mother, who was, without a doubt, the hardest-working person I knew. Every single day, she poured her heart and soul into providing for us, stretching herself far beyond what most people would ever consider doing. During the day, she ran a driving school, navigating the chaos of Dubai's streets at the hands of student drivers. At night, she worked shifts at Burger King. And in whatever slivers of time she could find between those two jobs, she hustled in real estate, trying to make ends meet. She worked eighteen to twenty hours a day, with barely any time to rest. The cost of living in Dubai was brutal, and every penny mattered. She was the first to arrive and the last to leave, always pushing herself beyond exhaustion, because she had no other choice.

But one night, everything shifted. She came home after yet another grueling day, but this time, something was different. I could see it in her face. There was a heaviness in her walk and a sadness in her eyes. She had been mistreated—again—by yet another business partner who had taken advantage of her kindness. This was not the first time someone had betrayed her trust, but this time, the phoenix energy I was used to from her wasn't there. She looked at me and, with all the weight of the world on her shoulders, asked, "Why is this happening? Why does everything have to be so hard?"

Hearing those words from my mother hit me harder than anything I had experienced up to that point. This woman, the strongest person I knew, was broken. She had raised me almost entirely on her own, abandoned by family members who did not take her seriously because she was a woman. They thought she could not rise above her circumstances. And the world treated her the same way—constantly underestimating her, taking advantage of her kindness, and pushing her to the margins. Whenever she did come out successful, her relatives and business partners were always knocking on her door, expecting a free handout. The only world my mother had known until this point had tried to take from her whatever self-esteem or success she had.

That night, as I watched my mother's once unbreakable spirit finally crack, something inside me shattered too. Her eyes, usually filled with fire, were now dulled by the weight of endless sacrifice and betrayal. For the first time in my life, I saw her as tired—truly defeated—and it terrified me. I couldn't stand it. The woman who had raised me on her own, who had defied everyone's expectations, was questioning why she had to keep fighting. And I swore to myself that night, with my heart pounding and my voice trembling, that I would change our fate. I would make sure no one ever looked down on us again and that one day everyone would know the name Zahedi.

Rejection Is Fuel

The idea that some people come into this world destined for success is a complete myth. I was not born into wealth, privilege, or any kind of advantage. I did not have a family business handed to me or someone opening doors for me. I was flipping burgers, cleaning offices, and taking any job that would help me survive. I was stuck in jobs that barely covered the bills, doing everything I could just to scrape by. But I made the decision that I was not going to live like that forever.

> **Here is the truth that no one wants to admit: Hard work alone will not make you successful.**

Here is the truth that no one wants to admit: Hard work alone will not make you successful. You can put in all the effort you want, but if you are doing it for someone else, you are still working toward their dream, not yours. I learned that the hard way. When my boss at Burger King rejected my request for a raise, I decided that I had to start building something for myself.

Entrepreneurship is not an easy path, and it does not happen overnight, but it's the only way to achieve real freedom. The truth is, all those people known as "natural-born entrepreneurs" did not get there because of destiny—they got there because they made a choice. They chose to take risks, to fail, and to keep pushing forward when others would have given up. That's the real difference between those who succeed and those who do not.

> **Entrepreneurship is not an easy path, and it does not happen overnight, but it's the only way to achieve real freedom.**

People are terrified of rejection. They take it as a personal defeat, as if it is a sign that they are not good enough. But I see it as an opportunity to get better, to refine my approach, and to learn something valuable.

Every no I hear becomes fuel for my fire. It pushes me to work smarter. Rejection is inevitable in entrepreneurship. You're going to hear no more times than you can count, whether it's from investors, customers, or even your friends and family. But every no teaches you something new—about your strategy, your timing, or even the way you pitch your idea. Don't take it personally; take it professionally. Analyze it, adapt, and come back stronger. That's how you turn rejection from an obstacle into an advantage.

Power Moves: Turn Rejection into Advantage

Rejection's not the end—it's an opportunity to make strategic power moves that take you even further. Here's how to turn each no into your next big win:

Move 1: Reframe the Setback
Instead of taking it personally, ask, "What lesson can I take from this?"

Move 2: Analyze the Play
Take a step back and figure out why things didn't go your way. Was it bad timing? The wrong opportunity? Pinpoint the issue so you can adapt and improve your next move.

Move 3: Improve Your Strategy
Now that you've spotted the problem, refine your approach. Whether it means sharpening your skills, refining your pitch, or building stronger relationships, step up your game.

Move 4: Adjust Your Next Move
Rejection isn't the endgame—it's a pivot. Use what you've learned to adjust your approach. Maybe target a new market or brainstorm a fresh idea.

> **Move 5: Play to Win**
> Rejection doesn't define you—your response does. Get back in the game with confidence, and use what you've learned from rejection to push forward. Your next win's just around the corner.

Rejection doesn't define you—your response does. Get back in the game with confidence, and use what you've learned from rejection to push forward. Your next win's just around the corner.

Small Choices That Lead to Big Results

One of the biggest misconceptions about success is that it happens because of some big, life-changing moment. People imagine it is one lucky break or a serendipitous opportunity. But that's normally not how it works. Success is built on small, daily decisions. It is the tiny choices you make every single day that add up to something bigger. When I was working those low-paying jobs, I could have stayed comfortable. I could have thought, *This is life. This is just how things are.* Instead, every day, I made the decision to keep moving forward. I asked myself, "What can I do today that will bring me closer to where I want to be?"

Those small choices—waking up early, staying late, taking on extra work—were not glamorous. But they added up over time. Every choice you make when no one is watching is an opportunity to move closer to your goals. It is easy to look at successful people and think they made one big leap to get where they are. But it is not about that one leap—it is about the hundreds of little steps that led to that moment.

Instead of waiting for the big opportunity, start focusing on what you can do every day to get closer to your goal. Whether it is learning something new, networking, or simply getting up early and putting in extra work, those little steps compound over time and create momentum. Success does not happen overnight—it is built one small step at a time.

> **It is easy to look at successful people and think they made one big leap to get where they are. But it is not about that one leap—it is about the hundreds of little steps that led to that moment.**

And here is the truth that not everyone is ready to hear: If you are stuck in your life, it's because you have not made the decision to change. It's easy to blame your circumstances, your boss, or your past. But at the end of the day, everything in your life is your responsibility. You cannot sit around waiting for someone to come along and hand you a better life. You have to go out and take it. Change is uncomfortable—I get that. But what is worse? Being uncomfortable for a little while, or waking up ten or twenty years from now, stuck in the same place, wondering where your dreams went? If you want something different, you have to make a choice. You have to take action. No one is going to make those choices for you. No one is going to come and save you. If you want to change your life, you have to be the one to do it. It is not easy, and it is not quick, but it is absolutely worth it.

The Decision That Defines You

I was not born an entrepreneur. I became one the day I made the decision to stop working for someone else and start building something of my own. You don't need someone's permission to succeed—you give yourself that permission. So if you want to build something great, start today. Make the choice, take the action, and begin to build. Every decision you make, every step you take, brings you closer to the life you want. And remember, you control how quickly you get there.

I was not born an entrepreneur. I became one the day I made the decision to stop working for someone else and start building something of my own.

So, what's stopping you from taking control? You don't need anyone's permission to start. You don't need special connections or a golden opportunity handed to you. All you need is the decision—the decision to grind, to persevere, and to build something of your own. The moment you decide to act, you're already an entrepreneur. Don't wait for someone else to believe in you—believe in yourself and get started today.

The moment you decide to act, you're already an entrepreneur. Don't wait for someone else to believe in you—believe in yourself and get started today.

Maverick Takeaways

- Success lies in your daily decisions and actions.
- It's not the most talented who succeed, but the most persistent.
- Every no you hear is an opportunity to sharpen your skills and improve your strategy.
- Working for someone else will never give you the freedom or success you're chasing.
- Identifying problems in your work environment is the first step to becoming a successful entrepreneur.
- It's not about a single breakthrough—it's about making consistent choices that move you closer to your goals.

CHAPTER FIVE

Grit over Luck

Conventional thought: A great idea is nothing without luck.

Maverick truth: We create our own luck with grit.

How the Relentless Outlast the Fortunate

They'll call it luck, every time. Every achievement, every breakthrough, every success you've fought for—they'll chalk it up to some invisible fortune shining down on you. But deep down, you'll know the truth: It wasn't luck. It was grit.

It wasn't luck. It was grit.

Success is a slow grind that happens while the rest of the world is still asleep. The people who rise aren't the ones who catch a lucky break—they're the ones who refuse to quit, who keep pushing when everything is falling apart. They're the ones who build their own destiny with sweat, persistence, and unrelenting determination.

Showing up and doing the work is another four-letter word that's become a big part of my vocabulary: *grit*. Grit in construction is the material used in cement to prevent cracks under pressure, and grit in life is what keeps you pushing forward when obstacles threaten your success. When you have grit, you have the strength to build something that lasts. Here are some other words that come to mind when I think of *grit*:

resilience	endurance	stamina
determination	resolve	drive
perseverance	toughness	persistence
tenacity	steadfastness	discipline
fortitude	mental toughness	

Grit Keeps Your Wheels on the Ground

My lessons in grit started early. I was twelve years old, living in a small apartment in government housing in Hoofddorp with my mom, who was doing everything she could to make ends meet. I watched my friends, who had parents with two solid incomes, receive everything they wanted: new sneakers, movie tickets, snacks from the corner store. They could just ask Mom and Dad for money, and without a second thought, it was handed to them. In contrast, I watched my mother work day and night to keep a roof over our heads, which made me never want to ask her for more. If I wanted these little luxuries that my friends had, I was determined to pay for them myself.

Because of my young age, the work options were limited, but there was one job I could do that many older teenagers growing up in Holland ended up doing: delivering newspapers. Believe it or not, I would wake up at 3:30 a.m. every single morning, long before anyone else was awake, and even before the sun had risen. I remember my alarm blaring in what felt like the middle of the night, calling me out of sleep. Every muscle in my body would want to keep snoozing, but I'd drag myself out of bed, dress in the dark, and quietly leave the apartment, trying not to wake my mother. Outside, the cold, damp air would hit me hard. My bike, an old, worn-out thing with a crooked frame, leaned against the building where I lived. I'd strap the newspaper bundles onto the back and ride through the empty streets, the only sound the quiet hum of my tires against the wet pavement.

The first few days were brutal. But staying focused on the end result kept me going. Every cold, predawn morning, as I pedaled through the silent streets of Amsterdam, I wasn't just fighting the elements; I was fighting for a better future. The wind would bite at my skin, and my hands felt like ice gripping the handlebars. Some mornings, the rain would pour down so hard that I could barely see the road. But I'd keep going. Every pedal felt like a step toward freedom—toward earning what I wanted without having to ask my mother for help. And in the silence of those early hours, with only the hum of my bike beneath me, I learned the most valuable lesson of my life: No one was coming to save me. If I wanted something, I had to work for it, day after day, no matter how exhausted or defeated I felt.

I knew that no one else was going to earn this money for me. Even when I was tired, even when it was pouring rain, even when I'd go home from school exhausted and every part of me wanted to quit, I persevered. It wasn't luck that kept me delivering newspapers in the freezing rain. It wasn't luck that kept me waking up before the sun, day after day. My experience delivering newspapers would shape my outlook for years to come. It taught me what it takes to get through tough times, how to push through discomfort, and, most importantly, how to keep going when there's no visible reward in sight.

Grit Keeps You Moving

A few years ago, the real estate market in Europe started to feel too limiting. Land and properties were too expensive, income taxes too high, and the bureaucracy around borrowing money too complicated. The general mindset of German real estate investors was extremely passive. They bought a property to hold on to it for a good ten years before even considering selling it. I knew I needed to play on a bigger stage, and I knew the United States was where I had to be if I wanted to scale up and reach the next level. I set a course: I saved up, hired the best lawyers, and began working on securing an E-2 visa. Just as all of my plans seemed to be falling into place, the Trump administration's travel ban went into effect. Suddenly, my visa application, which should have been a simple process, was denied. Even though I had lived most of my life in Europe and held a Dutch passport, the US government still classified me as Iranian because of my place of birth. And Iran just happened to be one of the newly blacklisted countries.

I was on the cusp of something great. I could feel it. After years of building my business in Europe, I knew that the United States was my next stage. I had poured my heart, soul, and capital into preparing for the move. The paperwork was filed, the lawyers were hired—it was all happening. Until it wasn't.

Receiving the visa rejection letter felt like a sucker punch to the gut. The words blurred on the page as I read that I'd been denied because of my Iranian birthplace, despite my Dutch citizenship. The door I had worked so hard to open was slammed shut, and to make matters worse, the pandemic hit. Borders were closing, economies were stalling, and my dream of expanding to the United States felt like it was crumbling before my eyes.

But grit doesn't let you sit in defeat for too long. It pulls you back up and pushes you to find another way. I doubled down in Europe, buying more properties, flipping them, and building the resources I needed. By the time the United States reopened, I didn't just walk in—I charged in, armed with the capital and confidence to make serious moves. My dream wasn't handed to me. I built it, one hard-earned step at a time.

> **My dream wasn't handed to me. I built it, one hard-earned step at a time.**

How was I able to be so resilient in the face of challenge? Years of training. First, just as I did when I was twelve, I start my day early—at 4:00 a.m., before the world kicks into gear, before distractions such as emails, phone calls, or social media gobble up my attention. At that time of day, with just my thoughts and my coffee, I remind myself of why I do everything I do. I'm going after a vision that stretches ten, twenty, thirty years ahead into the future. I'm building something bigger than myself, and that takes work—work that won't wait for anyone who wants to sleep in. That early time is sacred. I use it to focus on my goals, plan the day ahead, and get my head in the right place. Here's what I've learned: Grit is about showing up like this for myself each day and being my own best employee. By the time most people are just starting their day, I've already punched in hours on my time card.

Going the Extra Mile

Sara Blakely, the founder of Spanx, is a true woman of grit. She kept pitching her idea, even when people told her no, again and again. It was her persistence that led to a chance meeting with a Neiman Marcus buyer, which made her business take off. Or take the story of KFC—Colonel Sanders was turned down by banks 1,009 times before one finally gave him a shot. That wasn't luck—that was grit.

I've had my own chance encounters that, thanks to determination, have led to unexpected opportunities. A few years ago, I was in Munich, scouting cars for a dealership I was running with a business partner. We spent hours looking at different cars, comparing prices, and trying to find a deal that would make the whole trip worthwhile. After an exhausting day with nothing at the end to show for it, we decided to grab something to eat at a small Italian restaurant and drown our sorrows in some excellent Bolognese sauce.

The place was tiny—just a few tables crammed together. My business partner and I found a spot next to an older couple and sat down. As we ate our pasta and chatted, I couldn't help but overhear the couple's conversation. The man was telling his wife about how they were losing their parking space at their apartment building and that he didn't know what to do with one of their cars. My mind started racing with possibilities. *What kind of car was it? Could it be worth something? What if I could get it for a good deal?*

I leaned over and politely asked the man about the car. He was surprised, but open to the conversation. It was an Audi A3, in excellent shape. I asked him if I could come by and take a look at it. The next morning, I drove 160 kilometers all the way back to Munich. I inspected the car, ran the numbers in my head, and made him an offer on the spot. The man accepted, and just like that, I had bought the car for $7,000 under market value. A few weeks later, I flipped it for a solid profit.

When I told my business partner about the deal, he couldn't believe it. "Man, you got lucky with that one," he said. But I knew it wasn't luck. Someone else might have overheard that same conversation in the

Italian restaurant, shrugged their shoulders, and done nothing. Someone else may have started the conversation with the older man but then balked at the idea of having to drive back all that distance again. But I had made the choice to speak up, ask the right questions, and go the extra mile—or miles, in this case.

You never know when your next opportunity will come, but you'll always know if you were ready to grab it. So, the next time opportunity whispers in your ear, don't wait. Don't hesitate. Make your move, and make it count.

> **You never know when your next opportunity will come, but you'll always know if you were ready to grab it.**

Practical Steps to Building Grit

1. **Dare to do the work consistently.**
   Every day, show up for yourself. No shortcuts, no excuses. Invest the hours, and watch how the world starts to open doors that others will call "luck."
2. **Challenge yourself to build real relationships.**
   Success isn't a solo mission. Surround yourself with people who push you to be better, who help you see opportunities, and who are in it for the long haul.
3. **Embrace the humility of lifelong learning.**
   If you think you've got it all figured out, you're already behind. Stay open, stay curious, and never stop growing.

continued

> 4. **Step up to bold, calculated risks.**
>   If you're not afraid, you're not pushing hard enough. Take that leap, and watch as new opportunities appear where others only saw risk.
> 5. **Refuse to quit—especially when it's hard.**
>   The world is full of people who give up at the first sign of trouble. Don't be most people. Be the one who keeps going, no matter what.

Failing Forward: The Power of Persistence

Character is forged in the fires of failure. It's during those moments when everything seems to be crumbling that we learn our greatest lessons. The car dealership I opened with my business partner was not the success I had hoped for, but it turned out to be something even better: a failure I could learn from.

When we first started out, the business appeared to be doing well. Cars were moving off the lot quickly, money was coming in, and our reputation was growing. Everything seemed to be running smoothly. But then life threw me a curveball: My mother fell ill, and I had to step away from the business to be by her side. I trusted my partner to handle things in my absence, confident that he could manage since I'd taught him everything he needed to know—how to find the right cars, how to negotiate deals, how to close them. These things I had learned from past trial and error and from doing what most people avoid: a lot of research.

Character is forged in the fires of failure.

I wasn't just relying on experience; I put in the time to learn. Instead of wasting hours on social media, I used the internet to dive deep into best practices for car sales, pricing strategies, and negotiation techniques. On top of that, I personally visited dozens of dealerships, acting like I was going to buy a car, just to see their behavior, analyze their pitch, and understand their approach. I studied how they built rapport with customers, handled objections, and closed deals. Everything I absorbed during those visits I applied to our business. But still, life has a way of testing even the best-laid plans.

Every evening after spending time with my mother at the hospital, I'd swing by the dealership to check on our progress. The city would be quiet by then, the lights dim in the showroom, and everything appeared normal. Then one night, I noticed something unusual—new cars in the lot that I didn't recognize. *He must have made a few deals while I was gone*, I thought, trying to ignore the strange feeling in the pit of my stomach. Business was continuing, and that was what mattered, right?

But then it happened again. And again. Every night I came by, there were new cars. The strangest part was that our profit margins didn't reflect these new acquisitions. Something wasn't adding up. Still, I wanted to believe that everything was okay. My mind was occupied with my mother's health, and the last thing I needed was to stress over the business. I told myself not to jump to conclusions, to trust the person I had put so much faith in, who had been with me from the beginning.

But my gut wouldn't let it go. It gnawed at me until, one evening, I decided to stop by the dealership unexpectedly, past midnight. The showroom was dark, but the lot was full of unfamiliar cars. That's when I realized: The man I had trusted, my partner, had been making deals behind my back.

I started looking into our records, beginning with the car log—a simple paper trail where we documented the details of every car we had, from when they were purchased to how much we paid for them. But the new cars I kept seeing at the lot weren't listed anywhere. My next step was to check our bank accounts, comparing sales and purchases against the car inventory. That's when the red flags really started popping up. Our transactions didn't reflect the inventory, and sales seemed to be grinding to a halt.

I asked one of my close friends, who also worked at the dealership, if he knew what was going on. He claimed to have no idea but mentioned that sales had dropped to almost nothing. The situation was getting out of hand, so I finally confronted my partner. His response was nervous and evasive, and he suggested we meet the next day to "clear things up."

When we finally sat down the following day, he spun me a story about how those new cars belonged to his dad and he was simply doing him a favor by selling them. It didn't sit right with me, but I let it slide for the moment. Two weeks passed, and then I got a call from our landlord: The rent hadn't been paid, and he was giving us a week to settle it or he'd cancel the lease. Things were unraveling fast.

To get to the bottom of it, I sent two people to the dealership, undercover, pretending they were interested in buying cars. I told them to focus on our inventory and see how my partner responded. Both times, he steered them away from our cars, saying they were sold or unavailable, and pushed them toward his own cars instead. That was it. I confronted him with the evidence, but he had nothing to say. The betrayal was deeper than I had imagined. My friend, whom I thought I could count on, disappeared the moment I asked if he would back me in court. Turns out, he was in on it too.

We were forced to close the dealership after months of not making any money. I sued my partner, but it was too late. He filed for bankruptcy, leaving me with nothing to recover. That failure, as painful as it was, taught me a hard but invaluable lesson: Trust is fragile, and even the best-laid plans can be dismantled by deceit. But it didn't break me—it made me sharper and more resilient for the future.

Looking back, that failure taught me two versions of the same valuable lesson: (1) Never rely too much on a single individual, and (2) never build a business that hinges solely on my presence. If I hadn't been burned, I wouldn't have learned the importance of establishing systems and safeguards.

The Grit Blueprint: A Fourteen-Day Challenge for Building Mental Toughness

This two-week challenge is designed to develop habits that strengthen your mental resilience, sharpen your focus, and drive consistent progress, no matter the obstacles. Commit to it fully, and watch your endurance and determination make you and your business unstoppable.

DAYS 1–3: THE FOUNDATION OF GRIT

Shift Your Wake-Up Time to One Hour Earlier

Waking up an hour earlier creates an uninterrupted time to reflect on your long-term goals, connect with your core motivations, and plan the day ahead. It's a sacred time when you can think clearly without the noise of your partner, your children, business responsibilities, or social media. Take this time to solidify your vision, and begin each day with a clear purpose.

Embrace Physical Challenges to Push Your Limits

Begin each morning with a physical challenge—whether it's a cold shower, an intense run, or lifting weights. This simple habit forces your mind and body to confront discomfort and powers your mental toughness throughout the day. When you can push through physical resistance, you teach yourself to overcome mental blocks, too.

Tackle the Hardest Task Before 9:00 a.m.
The hardest part of your day is often the one you're most tempted to avoid. Whether it's a tough conversation, a major project, or a personal challenge, face it head-on, and do it early. Accomplishing this sets a victorious tone for the rest of the day and builds confidence in your ability to handle difficult tasks.

DAYS 4-6: PROGRESS WITH NO EXCUSES
Eliminate All Excuses

For the next three days, practice cutting out every excuse. Whenever you find yourself rationalizing or procrastinating—stop. Do what needs to be done without delay. Excuses are the enemy of discipline, and training yourself to act without them builds the discipline you need for long-term resilience. Stick to your commitments, no matter how small.

> **Excuses are the enemy of discipline, and training yourself to act without them builds the discipline you need for long-term resilience. Stick to your commitments, no matter how small.**

Seek Daily Discomfort

Intentionally place yourself in uncomfortable situations. Whether it's learning a new skill, engaging in a difficult conversation, or physically pushing your body, discomfort is where growth happens. The more you expose yourself to these moments, the more you build adaptability and mental toughness.

Fail at Something and Try Again

Set a task just outside your current abilities and expect to fail on the first attempt. The goal isn't to avoid failure but to learn from it, get back up, and try again until you succeed. This is the essence of persistence, and failure is a critical part of any meaningful progress. Each attempt strengthens your resolve.

DAYS 7–9: HARNESS SELF-REFLECTION AND ADAPTABILITY

Keep a Grit Journal

At the end of each day, document how you persevered through challenges. Write about the moments when you wanted to give up but didn't, and reflect on how those decisions shaped your day. Journaling helps track progress and offers a moment of personal accountability to reinforce your commitment to grit.

Use Reflection to Sharpen Your Awareness

Reflection goes beyond just documenting progress—it sharpens your self-awareness. Set time aside to evaluate your actions, your thoughts, and where you need to adjust. Regular reflection provides clarity and the insight to pivot when necessary, allowing you to stay aligned with your long-term goals while navigating setbacks.

Commit to Daily Progress

Regardless of how small the steps may feel, move the needle forward each day. Momentum comes from consistent effort, and progress compounds over time. Keep your focus on daily actions that build toward your long-term vision, and learn to appreciate the small wins. Over time, this commitment to progress will carry you through uncertainty.

DAYS 10–12: BUILD UNWAVERING FOCUS AND RELATIONSHIPS

Unplug for One Hour Every Day

Disconnect from all technology—phones, computers, and distractions—for one hour. Use this time to read, strategize, or engage in deep work that requires your full attention. This practice trains your mind to concentrate on what truly matters, without interruptions, and allows you to regain focus in a distracted world.

Train Yourself to Think Long Term

Short-term setbacks often derail people from their bigger vision. Dedicate these days to training your mind to focus beyond the dopamine rush of immediate results. Cultivate patience and resilience by keeping your long-term goals in view, even when daily outcomes aren't what you hoped for. Grit means thinking far beyond today's successes or failures.

> **Grit means thinking far beyond today's successes or failures.**

Curate an Environment of Excellence

Take stock of your relationships and environment. Surround yourself with people who challenge you to grow, hold you accountable, and push you toward excellence. Having a supportive, high-performing network is essential for staying on track when self-doubt creeps in. These people will keep you focused and help you see opportunities you might otherwise miss.

DAYS 13-14: REJUVENATE AND REFLECT ON YOUR JOURNEY

Prioritize Strategic Rest and Recovery

High performance doesn't mean constant action—it requires periods of recovery. Use these final two days to rest, recharge, and reflect. Take time to spend with family, enjoy personal hobbies, or engage in activities that bring you peace. This rest period prevents burnout and ensures you're mentally and physically ready for the next challenge.

Reflect on Your Grit Journey

Look back over the past fourteen days and evaluate your progress. What challenges did you overcome? Where did you struggle? How did you push through discomfort, and what did you learn from your failures? This reflection helps you integrate the lessons learned and prepare for the next phase of your journey.

> **Each challenge, each small victory, and each failure build your resilience.**

As you've seen from this chapter, building grit isn't about one massive effort—it's about showing up day after day, the way I did for my paper route when I was twelve. Each challenge, each small victory, and each failure build your resilience. The habits you've cultivated during these two weeks—eliminating excuses, embracing discomfort, reflecting on your progress—are the foundation for long-term success.

People might see my success now and think I got lucky, but what they don't see are the years of struggle, the sleepless nights, and the sheer determination to make it through. Luck didn't get me here. Grit did. The same principle applies to anyone striving to achieve something great.

Now it's your turn. What will you do with the time you have? Will you wait for luck, or will you take the reins and create your own destiny? Remember: Those who wait for luck often wait forever. Those who build with grit always find a way.

> **Remember: Those who wait for luck often wait forever. Those who build with grit always find a way.**

Maverick Takeaways

- Success isn't about catching a lucky break; it's built brick by brick with relentless effort, persistence, and a refusal to quit.

- Show up every day, regardless of how you feel. Those who put in the work, day after day, create their own opportunities.

- Just like grit in cement prevents cracks, personal grit holds you together when challenges threaten your success.
- When you keep pushing through obstacles, what others call "luck" is really the outcome of your persistence and effort.
- Embrace your setbacks. Every failure teaches you a lesson and adds to your mental toughness for future challenges.
- Nobody's coming to save you. Your grit, determination, and daily efforts are what carve out your path to success.

CHAPTER SIX

Mastering Money: Control Wealth, Command Freedom

Conventional thought: Money makes you a slave to greed.

Maverick truth: Mastering money is the key to freedom.

Many of us grow up hearing that often-quoted Bible verse: "Money is the root of all evil." In Germany, where I live, wealth is frequently associated with the worst of human traits: greed, corruption, and exploitation. For others, money is something to be feared or endlessly chased, but never something that can be truly controlled. For a long time, I shared these beliefs. To me, money was merely a means of survival—a tool to pay bills, buy essentials, and, occasionally, if I was lucky, splurge on something small. I was stuck in a cycle of earning and spending, with no real thought given to the long-term potential of my financial decisions.

But that all changed when I reached a significant financial milestone in my life, one that forced me to stop and reconsider everything I thought I knew about wealth. When I turned twenty-one, everything shifted. Up until that point, money had always been about survival—paying bills, covering necessities, scraping by just enough to get to the next day. But then, I saved my first $100,000. For the first time, I didn't just have enough to get by—I had more. It was my first taste of financial freedom. I realized that wealth gave me control over my time, my decisions, and, ultimately, my future. With that six-figure number staring back at me in my account, I felt a spark of clarity. I wasn't just surviving anymore; I was finally living on my own terms.

It was in that moment that I realized my understanding of money had been flawed. I came to understand that true wealth wasn't the end goal, but the gateway to growth, independence, and lasting impact, both for myself and for the people around me. This shift in perspective changed everything for me, and from that point forward, I began to see money as a means to build something greater than what I could see.

I came to understand that true wealth wasn't the end goal, but the gateway to growth, independence, and lasting impact, both for myself and for the people around me.

More Than Just Numbers: When Wealth Isn't About Buying More

In the early years of my career, I was constantly focused on survival. Money, for me, was something to be earned and spent as quickly as it came in. I lived in a cycle of financial stress—there was always a bill to pay, an expense to cover, a looming deadline that meant more financial obligations. My mindset was transactional. I didn't think beyond the next paycheck, and my goals were small, focused on immediate needs and occasional indulgences. I remember vividly the time when being able to afford a new suit felt like a monumental victory.

But now that I had some savings in the bank, I could confidently say that I no longer had to chase money as my primary driver. I had reached a level where I could afford to focus on what really mattered to me—building a legacy, making a name that would last, and creating something that would outlive me. I was forced to take a step back and really think about what I was doing. Why was I chasing after money? What was it for?

One of the most pivotal moments in this journey was when I decided to stop working as a contractor and work for myself instead. Up until that point, I had been saving and spending my money like everyone else—putting some away for a rainy day and then spending the rest on the things I thought I needed. But when I made the decision to invest in my business, everything changed. I began to see my money multiply in ways that simple saving never could. Instead of just accumulating wealth, I was building something that had the potential to create long-term value, not just for myself but for others as well.

Another key moment came when I realized that money could buy me time—time to focus on the things I loved, to spend with the people who mattered most to me, and to pursue passions that had nothing to do with financial gain. Money gave me the freedom to say no to the things that drained my energy and yes to the opportunities that aligned with my purpose. This was a profound shift in how I thought about wealth. It wasn't about accumulating more; it was about creating freedom.

When I stopped chasing money for the sake of material gains and started seeing it as a means to create freedom and options, I was able to break free from the scarcity mindset that had held me back for so long. I began thinking long term, focusing on how to grow wealth in a sustainable, impactful way rather than simply accumulating it.

Another key moment came when I realized that money could buy me time—time to focus on the things I loved, to spend with the people who mattered most to me, and to pursue passions that had nothing to do with financial gain.

Moreover, I began to see the ripple effect that money could have when used wisely.

A few years ago, my cousin came to me with a vision to start her own real estate agency. She had been working in the industry for years, building relationships and mastering the market, but she lacked the capital to take the leap and launch her own firm. I saw the potential in her plan and, more importantly, in her drive. I decided to invest in her dream, providing the initial funds for office space, licensing, and marketing. Watching her agency grow from a small operation to one of the most respected in the area was incredible. Knowing that my financial support helped her create something lasting was more fulfilling than any investment I'd ever made.

Watching my cousin succeed, knowing that my financial support had helped her create something of her own, proved that wealth, when shared wisely, can have a ripple effect. It's not just about you—it's about how you can leverage your financial power to uplift others, create opportunities, and contribute to something larger than yourself.

Success Isn't Selling Out: Balancing Wealth with Integrity

Throughout my career, I've seen countless entrepreneurs struggle to reconcile their pursuit of wealth with maintaining their integrity and values. This is a common challenge, particularly when financial success brings temptations that test your core principles. I've faced those moments myself, and I want to share a few insights that have helped me navigate them.

In the early stages of my career, I was like many driven entrepreneurs—hungry for success, determined to make a name for myself, and relentlessly focused on growth. I poured my heart, my soul, and every penny I had into my business. For years, I lived in constant survival mode, making sacrifices that most people wouldn't even consider—sleeping in my office, working twenty-hour days, and skipping family events in the hope that one day it would all pay off.

And then it did. One day, the breakthrough came—a huge contract that catapulted my company into the multimillion-dollar range. Suddenly, I was no longer struggling to keep the lights on. I was running a thriving empire. The money flowed in, the recognition started, and my name began to carry weight in business circles. But with this success came new challenges.

One particular challenge arose when I was presented with a business opportunity that promised significant financial gains—potentially tens of millions of dollars. On paper, it looked perfect. The deal would take my company to the next level, cementing my place among the elite. But there was a catch. To secure the deal, I would have to compromise my values—cut corners, overlook questionable business practices, and engage in behavior that went against the very principles that had guided me from the start.

It was an agonizing decision. I was at a crossroads, a point every entrepreneur faces at some stage. On one hand, there was the allure of exponential growth and the prospect of achieving financial security beyond my wildest dreams. On the other, there was my integrity—the moral compass that had guided me from my humble beginnings.

I thought back to those early days, remembering why I had started my business in the first place. It wasn't just for the money. It was to build something meaningful, something that would stand the test of time—a legacy, a name that would be remembered. I realized that if I compromised my values now, everything I had built would be on shaky ground. Success at the cost of integrity, I knew, was no success at all. It would be fleeting and hollow and, worse, tarnish my name.

In the end, I walked away from the deal. It wasn't easy. I faced criticism and lost potential partners, and for a while, it seemed like I had made the wrong decision. But over time, that choice paid off in ways that went far beyond money. My company grew, not because of shortcuts or compromises but because of the strength of my reputation. Clients trusted me, partners respected me, and my name—Zahedi—became synonymous with integrity and excellence.

For entrepreneurs who struggle to reconcile their pursuit of wealth with their values, here's the advice I would give:

- Know your nonnegotiables. Before you ever get caught in a tough decision, identify the core values you refuse to compromise on, no matter what. For me, it was honesty, fairness, and a commitment to doing business the right way. These values became my anchor, guiding me through both the good times and the bad. When you know where you stand, the right decision becomes clearer, even in the face of tempting financial rewards.

- Remember that success without integrity is temporary. It's easy to get caught up in the rush of a big payday or the allure of rapid growth, but without a strong ethical foundation, those victories are fleeting. I learned that while compromising my values might have brought quick wins, it would have eroded the long-term trust and respect I had worked so hard to build. The entrepreneurs who stand the test of time are the ones who value their reputation over a quick buck.

Remember that success without integrity is temporary. It's easy to get caught up in the rush of a big payday or the allure of rapid growth, but without a strong ethical foundation, those victories are fleeting.

- Play the long game. Wealth can come and go, but your name is what lasts. My goal was never just to make money; it was to build a legacy that would be remembered. I understood that in the end, it wasn't about being the richest person in the room—it was about being the most respected. By staying true to my values, I ensured that my name would endure, long after the deals and dollars faded.

- Don't be afraid to walk away. There will be times when the most lucrative opportunities come with the highest moral cost. In those moments, walking away can feel like a loss, but it's actually a win for your character and your future. I learned that the deals you say no to are just as important as the ones you say yes to.

Play the long game. Wealth can come and go, but your name is what lasts.

Entrepreneurship is a relentless pursuit of growth, innovation, and, yes, wealth. But wealth without integrity is a fragile thing. For me, the challenges, failures, and tough decisions only strengthened my resolve. The money came, but more importantly, so did the reputation I had always dreamed of. Entrepreneurs, take heart—your values are your greatest asset. Protect them fiercely, and the rewards will follow in ways you never imagined.

You Call It *Success*; I Call It *Discipline*

Over the years, I have developed several key systems and habits that have helped me stay disciplined and responsible with money while avoiding the traps of greed or superficiality. Like many entrepreneurs, I've faced the temptation of chasing quick wins and falling into the allure of money for money's sake. But I've learned that true financial success doesn't come from constantly pursuing more; it comes from mastering discipline and focusing on what matters.

TREAT MONEY AS A TOOL, NOT A TROPHY

One of the first new mindsets I adopted was viewing money not as a measure of success, but as a tool to create freedom, impact, and opportunities. Early in my career, I caught myself attaching my self-worth to the numbers in my bank account. I realized that this was a dangerous trap—one that led to superficial goals and an endless chase for more without ever feeling fulfilled.

So, I made a deliberate shift. I started asking myself, "How can I use money to build something meaningful?" Whether it was investing in my business, supporting causes I care about, or helping others, I focused on using money to create lasting value. This shift in perspective helped me stay grounded and prevented money from becoming the end goal in itself.

AUTOMATE SAVING AND INVESTING

One of the most practical systems I put in place was automating my financial decisions. Early on, I made it a habit to automatically set aside a percentage of my income for savings and investments. I wanted to create a system that ensured my financial growth without having to make constant decisions. By automating this process, I removed the temptation to spend impulsively or chase flashy purchases.

LIVE BELOW YOUR MEANS, NO MATTER YOUR INCOME

As my wealth grew, I made a conscious decision to live below my means. It's easy to get caught up in lifestyle inflation—when you start earning more, you feel the pressure to spend more on bigger houses, flashier cars, or expensive experiences to "prove" your success. But I've always believed that true wealth is about freedom, not showing off.

Living below my means lets me focus on what I value most: financial independence, long-term security, and the ability to invest in projects that matter. This discipline has not only kept me grounded but also has allowed me to build a strong financial foundation without getting trapped in superficial pursuits. By controlling my spending, I free up resources to invest in meaningful ventures that align with my goals, not just my desires.

The Three-Month Financial Mastery Challenge

Here's a hands-on, unique, three-month challenge designed to completely shift the way you manage your money. It's structured to provide a deep understanding of your financial habits while helping you build discipline and long-term strategies.

Month 1: The Financial Cleanse

- Track every dollar.
- Separate business and personal finances.
- Create a cash flow statement.
- Set baseline financial metrics.

Month 2: The Profitability Shift

- Cut unnecessary expenses.
- Focus on profit, not revenue.
- Build a cash reserve.

Month 3: The Generosity and Investment Strategy

- Invest in education or skills.
- Automate your savings and investments.
- Generosity in action: Give back to your community.

Maverick Takeaways

- Wealth creates freedom and opportunities to build something lasting.

- Money may bring quick wins, but only those who prioritize their values build reputations that stand the test of time.

- Mastering money means buying back your time and freedom, not indulging in endless material pursuits.

- Real wealth is built by controlling spending and focusing on financial independence and long-term impact, not lifestyle inflation.

- Instead of saving for the sake of it, focus on investing in your business or ventures that create sustainable, long-term value.

- Sharing wealth and uplifting others expands your impact and creates a ripple effect beyond personal financial gains.

CHAPTER SEVEN

No Team, No Dream

Conventional thought:
Entrepreneurs are solopreneurs.

Maverick truth: Nobody
succeeds on their own.

The Fall of Superman

When I opened Barcode, my first nightclub, I was in full-on solopreneur mode. I had saved up every penny and poured it all into the business. I had also taken out loans, maxed out credit cards, and put myself in a situation where there was no turning back. The pressure was huge, and with that pressure came the belief that I had to control every single aspect of the business.

I had come up with the concept myself—every detail of it. I was the one who scouted the location, finding just the right spot that I believed would pull in the crowds. I obsessed over the decor, the vibe, the lighting, the sound—everything, down to the glasses we would use and the music we would play. I'd wake up before sunrise, filled with the anxiety of making sure everything was perfect, and I wouldn't stop working until well after the last clubber had left, usually sometime in the early hours of the morning. I managed the promotions, designing flyers, overseeing social media campaigns, and coming up with creative ways to keep people coming back. I even created the staff schedules, making sure every shift was covered and dealing with last-minute changes when someone couldn't make it in. It was the equivalent of working five jobs, and it was nuts.

At first, it felt exhilarating. There's something intoxicating about seeing a business you've built with your own hands begin to take shape. When the club filled up with people, when the music was thumping and the energy was electric, I'd look around and think, *I did this.* It was my hard work that brought those people in, my determination that made the club come to life. And that rush, that adrenaline, was addictive. It made all the long hours and sleepless nights feel worth it. I convinced myself that as long as I kept pushing, as long as I kept working harder than everyone else, success was just around the corner.

At the time, I saw this approach as a badge of honor. I thought that being "hands-on" meant I was doing what needed to be done to make the business a success. I prided myself on burning the candle at both ends and outworking everyone around me. I was the first one in and the last one out, every single day. And when I say I was involved in everything, I mean *everything*. If a glass broke in the middle of a busy night, I was the one sweeping it up. If the bartenders were slammed, I was behind the bar pouring drinks. But what I didn't realize was that I wasn't building an empire—I was running myself into the ground.

The nightclub was busier than ever, and while that should have been a good thing, it quickly became overwhelming. Suddenly, I wasn't just managing a small operation anymore—I was dealing with a packed house night after night, with all the challenges that come with that kind of success. But because I was still trying to do everything myself,

I couldn't keep up. I was missing important details, and my decision-making suffered. Problems that could have been easily avoided were slipping through the cracks because I was stretched too thin. The more I tried to control everything, the more control I actually lost. It wasn't just the business that was at risk—it was me. I was burning out, and fast.

I remember one particularly bad night, when everything seemed to go wrong at once. The sound system crashed right before a major event, leaving the DJ scrambling to get set up while the crowd grew impatient. The bar was running low on supplies because I had forgotten to place an order in time. Security was struggling to manage the line outside because we hadn't planned for such a large crowd. And where was I? Running around like a madman, trying to fix every problem at once, while my team stood by, unsure of what to do because I hadn't empowered them to take charge.

That night was a disaster—not because of any one thing, but because of a series of small, preventable mistakes that snowballed into a major issue. And it was all because I was clinging to the belief that I had to do it all myself. In trying to be a hero, I had become the bottleneck, the single point of failure. The very thing I thought made me strong—my insistence on handling everything—was what was dragging the business down.

I had to shift my thinking and accept that I wasn't Superman, and I couldn't do everything on my own, no matter how much I wanted to. There were people out there who were better than I was at certain things. It wasn't an easy realization. For someone who had prided himself on being a solopreneur, admitting that I couldn't do it all felt like a failure. But in reality, it was the best decision I ever made. The moment I started building a team and trusting others with parts of the business, things started to change.

> **I had to shift my thinking and accept that I wasn't Superman, and I couldn't do everything on my own, no matter how much I wanted to.**

I went to the quiet of my office to think. As I sat there, I reflected on everything that had gone wrong that night. It was clear: This giant mess was a culmination of my flawed approach to running the business. The sound system breaking down? That wasn't just a freak accident—it was a sign that I needed someone on staff whose sole responsibility was overseeing the tech. The bartenders being overwhelmed? It wasn't just about having enough drinks stocked—it was about management. I needed someone to oversee the bar operations: someone who could handle staffing, inventory, and customer flow on busy nights like this. And then there was the security issue. Having a short-staffed security team on a night like this wasn't just an inconvenience—it was dangerous. I needed someone whose full-time job was ensuring we had the right number of security personnel on duty every night, especially for major events.

That night was a turning point for me. I realized that if I wanted my business to succeed, I couldn't be the one doing everything. I had to build a team, a real team, made up of people who were experts in their areas and who could take the weight off my shoulders. It was one of the hardest yet most important lessons I would learn as an entrepreneur.

Here are some practical ways you can avoid the pitfalls of micromanaging.

STEP BACK AND EVALUATE

Ask yourself these questions to evaluate whether you're on the same unsustainable path I was on:

- Are you spending more time managing day-to-day tasks than focusing on growth?
- When was the last time you delegated something important? Reflect on whether you're holding on to tasks that could easily be managed by someone else.

RECOGNIZE YOUR BOTTLENECKS

The biggest lesson I learned that night was that by trying to do everything, I had become the bottleneck. I wasn't empowering my team, and they didn't have the autonomy to make decisions when things went wrong. Ask yourself:

- Which processes always seem to slow down because I'm the one in charge?
- Which tasks could someone else handle more efficiently than I could?

HIRE FOR YOUR WEAKNESSES

A key part of being a successful entrepreneur is recognizing that you can't be an expert in everything. It's essential to bring people onto your team who have strengths in areas where you're weak. Here are a few key roles you should consider delegating:

- Operations and logistics: manages the day-to-day, ensuring everything runs smoothly, and handles any issues that arise
- Finance: from budgeting to forecasting, makes sure your financial health is constantly monitored

- Marketing and promotions: brings fresh, creative ideas to the table and executes them
- Tech and maintenance: oversees technical issues, preventing equipment failures like the sound system breakdown

BUILD REDUNDANCY INTO YOUR TEAM

One of the biggest issues I faced was not having backup. To prevent this from happening in your business:

- Cross-train employees: Ensure that key staff are trained in multiple roles, so they can step in when needed.
- Create backup plans: Always have contingency plans for a major event, staffing shortages, or system failures.

FOCUS ON STRATEGY, NOT JUST OPERATIONS

As the owner, your most valuable contributions should come from high-level strategy, not the day-to-day grind. Ask yourself:

- Am I spending too much time putting out fires instead of planning for growth?
- What would happen to my business if I stepped away for a week?

Learning to Trust Your Team

The morning after that apocalyptic night at the club, I started building a team. To do this, I had to let go of my need to control everything, and I had to trust other people to take ownership of different aspects of the business. The first hire I made was a marketing manager, and honestly, it was the hardest. Marketing had always been my favorite part of the business. I loved coming up with promotions, planning events, and figuring out how to draw people in. But I knew I couldn't keep doing it all on my own.

I had to force myself to step back and let Vanessa, the new marketing manager, do her job. I gave her the freedom to experiment, try new strategies, and take risks that I wasn't comfortable with. And to my surprise, she ended up doing a much better job than I could have. She brought fresh ideas and new energy to the table that completely transformed our marketing efforts. Within a few months, we were attracting bigger crowds than I'd ever pulled in on my own.

The next key hire was a head bartender. I needed someone who understood not just how to make drinks but also how to create an experience. When I found Daniel, I knew he was the right fit. I gave him full control over the drink menu, and he came up with cocktails that became the talk of the town. Our bar went from being a sidenote to being a major attraction, where people knew the drinks were good, all because I trusted him to take it in a new direction.

Next came the security team. After the chaos of that Friday night, I knew we needed to tighten up our operations. I hired Ralph, a security manager whose entire focus was ensuring the safety of our guests and staff. He brought in new protocols, hired the right people, and created a system that ran smoothly, even on our busiest nights.

Trust doesn't come easily for a lot of entrepreneurs, and I was no different. In fact, I might have been worse than most. I was still holding on too tightly to the reins, checking in on every little thing, making sure everything was done "my way," because deep down, I didn't think anyone else could handle it. I'd look over someone's shoulder to see if the job was being done to my standards, I'd ask for constant updates, and I'd intervene the moment something didn't feel exactly right.

> **Trust doesn't come easily for a lot of entrepreneurs, and I was no different.**

Slowly but surely, I began to loosen my grip, and I started to see results. As I started to see my managers and staff succeed on their own, I realized I was empowering them to lead in their own way, to bring their own creativity and problem-solving skills to the table. That meant also giving them the power to take risks, to experiment, and to learn from their successes and failures.

That's when things really started to change for the better. Things were going so well that we had to start rejecting people at the door because we'd hit max capacity. The demand was insane. With my team's help, I had more time to strategize about expanding the business. I opened a second club just four minutes away, in the same city. The first club stayed open until 4:00 a.m., and the new one went until 5:00 a.m. (different permits). We'd shuffle guests between the two, giving people from the first club priority access to the second, keeping the energy high and ensuring no one left for a competitor. We used everything like vouchers, exclusive events, and DJ meet and greets to make sure our crowd stayed with us. We wanted people to keep coming back—and they did.

Of course, there were times when things didn't go perfectly. There were promotions that flopped, new cocktail ideas that didn't sell, and security measures that didn't work out the way we'd planned. But those things would have happened anyway with me acting as a solopreneur. They say with freedom comes responsibility. By allowing my team members the freedom to experiment and sometimes fail, I also was letting them invest themselves into the business and feel responsible for problem-solving. Now if things went crooked, there was a whole team of us to take charge and straighten them out.

> **They say with freedom comes responsibility. By allowing my team members the freedom to experiment and sometimes fail, I also was letting them invest themselves into the business and feel responsible for problem-solving.**

Contrarian Control Freak Rehab

Still can't give up control? Here are some out-of-the-box experiments to help you learn to trust your team:

- **Trust Thirty-Day Challenge: A Step-Back Experiment**
  For the next thirty days, pick one part of your business that you're still tightly controlling. Whether it's marketing, sales, or customer service, step back entirely, and let your team run it without your interference. Don't just delegate—completely detach yourself from it. At the end of the thirty days, analyze what went well, what didn't, and how stepping back affected the results.

- **Failure Celebration Day**
  Choose a day to celebrate failure. Have your team members share mistakes they've made and the lessons they've learned. Make failure a badge of honor, and encourage risk-taking by showing that mistakes are opportunities for growth. Reward those who took the biggest risks, even if they didn't work out, to reinforce the idea that innovation matters more than playing it safe.

- **The "CEO for a Day" Rotation**
  Each week, assign one of your team members to be the "CEO" for a day. Let them lead a meeting, make key decisions, and

continued

experience the pressure you face daily. This will not only build trust but also give them a clearer understanding of the big picture and foster leadership development.

- **Reverse Mentoring: Let Your Team Teach You**
  Set up regular "reverse mentoring" sessions where your team teaches you about their roles, new strategies, or skills they've developed. This practice builds trust by showing you value their expertise and gives them a sense of ownership in the business.
- **Weekly Vision-Alignment Challenge**
  Once a week, ask your managers or team leads to come up with one new idea that pushes the company toward your broader vision. You won't interfere in their process or decision—let them run with it. This reinforces trust while aligning their actions with long-term goals.

The Power of Collective Success

I remember watching my bartenders on busy nights, and it struck me that they were the face of the business. They were the ones who created the atmosphere, built relationships with our regulars, and set the tone for the entire experience. Without them, the club wouldn't have been the same. The same went for the marketing manager, who wasn't just coming up with generic ads but was constantly thinking of innovative ways to attract new clientele. And then there was the security team, who made sure that the environment remained safe and welcoming, allowing people to have a good time without worrying about anything going wrong. Every single member of the team contributed to the overall success, and each role was vital.

That's when I started to understand something that changed the way I approached not just the nightclub, but business in general: The business wasn't just mine anymore—it belonged to all of us. That shift in mindset made a world of difference. When your team feels like they're part of something bigger, when they know their contributions matter and they're not just cogs in a machine, everything changes. The energy is different, the passion is different, and the results are different. People stop coming to work just for a paycheck—they start coming because they believe in what they're building alongside you.

> **When your team feels like they're part of something bigger, when they know their contributions matter and they're not just cogs in a machine, everything changes.**

With the right team in place, I was able to do something I never thought was possible: I stepped back. Instead of spending every minute putting out fires, handling day-to-day operations, and making sure every detail was perfect, I was thinking strategically about the future. I had the mental space and the time to focus on growth—how to expand the business, how to reach new markets, how to take the nightclub to the next level.

I wasn't just stuck in the weeds anymore; I was thinking about the long-term vision, about what we could build together, not just what I could accomplish alone. And the business started to grow in ways I hadn't even considered possible before. We started taking things to the next level. Renting out shopping malls after-hours for eight-thousand-plus people became our norm. We hosted everything from open-air foam parties to massive pool parties at the biggest resort in town. We even began organizing mini-festivals, bringing in more than twelve DJs at a time to set the vibe. The boat parties were a game changer—we rented boats, cruised for four to six hours, and turned every ride into a wild experience. We were, in essence, redefining the way people experienced nightlife.

I was thinking beyond operations now and about how to build a brand that could expand into different markets and make the nightclub something bigger than just a single venue. And none of that would have been possible if I had tried to do it all myself. The collective effort of the team was what allowed us to dream bigger, push the boundaries, and achieve more than I ever could have imagined at the outset.

Together, our team was creating something far greater than the sum of its parts. That's when you stop being just a business owner and start being a leader. That's when your vision starts to become reality—not because you're doing all the work, but because you're surrounded by people who believe in that vision as much as you do. And that's when you start to see what's truly possible.

Alignment Leads to Legacy

Over the years, I've learned that clarity, communication, and consistency are the keys to keeping the team on track and ensuring that conflicts don't derail our progress. Following are some of the crucial steps to creating alignment that I've gleaned from my own experience.

> **Over the years, I've learned that clarity, communication, and consistency are the keys to keeping the team on track and ensuring that conflicts don't derail our progress.**

ESTABLISHING A CLEAR, COMMUNICATED VISION FROM DAY ONE

In my real estate ventures, from property development to investments, I've always made it a priority to ensure my team knows where we're headed long term. Whether it's building a portfolio of properties that prioritizes sustainable design or creating affordable housing with a focus on community, I make sure everyone on the team understands the "why" behind the work. If the entire team is aligned on this purpose, they're more likely to make decisions that support it.

For example, during a particularly ambitious project, we were developing a large mixed-use property. From the start, the goal was not just to build another set of commercial and residential units but to create a community space that would enhance the lives of the people living there. I made this vision clear in every meeting and every discussion—from the architects to the property managers. This ensured that everyone, from the construction teams to the sales agents, was aligned with the end goal.

Key strategy: Have regular, focused meetings where you reiterate the long-term vision. Don't assume people will remember it—reinforce it through real-world examples, project goals, and reminders of the bigger picture.

LEAD BY EXAMPLE AND SHOW LONG-TERM COMMITMENT

One of the most powerful ways I keep my team aligned is by leading by example. In real estate, especially when it comes to investments or developments that take years to complete, it's easy for teams to get caught up in the short-term tasks and lose sight of the bigger goal. As the leader, I make sure I'm demonstrating my commitment to the long-term vision in everything I do.

For example, during a period when the market was particularly volatile, some of my team members were getting nervous about short-term profitability and pushing for decisions that would compromise our long-term goals for quick wins. Instead of giving in to that pressure, I reminded the team of our commitment to quality and long-term value. I invested more of my own time to personally meet with our major partners and clients, ensuring them—and my team—that we were sticking to our vision, even during tough times. This act of reinforcing the bigger picture helped refocus everyone's efforts on sustainable growth rather than chasing short-term gains.

Key strategy: When things get tough, don't let short-term setbacks distract you or your team from the bigger vision. Show your long-term commitment through your decisions and actions, and your team will follow.

ALIGN INCENTIVES WITH THE LONG-TERM VISION

One of the ways I've learned to keep my real estate team aligned is by tying incentives to long-term success. It's not enough to tell people about your vision—you need to make sure their day-to-day efforts are rewarded in a way that reflects that vision. In real estate, this can be tricky, because there's often a focus on short-term milestones such as closing deals or filling vacancies.

At one point, I had a sales team focused purely on selling units in a high-end residential building we were developing. The problem was that, while they were hitting sales targets, they weren't being selective enough about the type of tenants we wanted to attract. We were trying to build a luxury brand, and some of the buyers didn't align with that vision. To fix this, I restructured the team's incentives, linking bonuses not only to sales numbers but also to the quality of the buyer and how well they fit with the brand we were building. This shifted the team's focus and helped keep them aligned with the long-term vision of creating a premium, high-end development.

Key strategy: Structure your team's incentives to reflect the long-term goals of the business. Whether it's tying bonuses to customer satisfaction, long-term tenant retention, or brand alignment, make sure the team is rewarded for contributing to the overall vision, not just immediate wins.

HANDLE CONFLICTS BY ADDRESSING THEM EARLY AND TRANSPARENTLY

Conflicts are inevitable in any business, especially in real estate, where there are so many moving parts—multiple stakeholders, fluctuating markets, tight deadlines, and high stakes. When conflicts arise, whether between team members, partners, or departments, the key is to address them early and transparently. Letting issues fester can lead to bigger problems down the road.

I remember a particularly challenging situation when we were developing a large commercial property. One of my key project managers and the head of construction had a serious disagreement about how to handle a zoning issue. The project manager wanted to push ahead without resolving the issue completely to meet deadlines, while the construction head insisted on a more cautious approach to avoid potential legal complications. This was a major conflict that could have derailed the entire project if left unchecked.

Instead of letting the disagreement escalate, I brought both parties together for a frank discussion. We laid everything on the table—the risks, the deadlines, the potential long-term effects of each approach. In the end, by facilitating open communication and focusing on the shared goal of delivering a successful project, we were able to reach a compromise. The zoning issue was resolved, but we adjusted timelines slightly to accommodate the more cautious approach, ultimately protecting the long-term vision for the project.

Key strategy: When conflicts arise, address them head-on. Create a space for open, transparent communication where the focus is on solving the problem, not on blaming individuals. Keep the conversation anchored to the long-term vision, and show how the conflict resolution will support that larger goal.

REGULARLY REVISIT AND ADJUST THE VISION

Real estate is a dynamic industry—markets change, client needs evolve, and new opportunities arise. To keep my team aligned, I make sure we regularly revisit the long-term vision and adjust it where necessary. I've learned that flexibility is essential. While the core of the vision may remain the same, the strategy for achieving it may need to evolve.

A perfect example is when we were developing a commercial real estate property right before the pandemic hit. The original vision was to create a series of coworking spaces and shared offices, which at the time was a booming market. But as the pandemic unfolded, the demand for coworking spaces plummeted, and we had to rethink the project's direction. Instead of stubbornly sticking to the old plan, I gathered the team, and we reevaluated the market. We decided to pivot, adjusting our long-term vision to focus on flexible office spaces with more private areas, which ended up being a better fit for the post-pandemic work environment.

This ability to adapt while staying true to the bigger picture allowed us to stay competitive and ultimately succeed in a challenging market.

Key strategy: Revisit your vision regularly, especially in fast-moving industries like real estate. Don't be afraid to pivot or adjust the strategy to stay aligned with market conditions. Involve your team in these discussions to keep everyone on the same page.

Maverick Takeaways

- Micromanaging kills your business. Empower your team to lead and succeed.
- Trying to do everything yourself will ultimately destroy both you and your business.
- Gradually delegate and allow your team to take ownership of their roles.
- Give your team room to make mistakes; every misstep is a stepping stone toward growth.
- Build a team invested in your vision, and you'll achieve far more than you could alone.
- The sooner you relinquish control, the sooner your business can scale beyond you.

CHAPTER EIGHT

Learning Never Stops: Adapt or Die

Conventional thought:
Success means you've arrived.

Maverick truth: Keep evolving,
or you're obsolete.

My First Lesson in Negotiation

I was eight years old, standing next to my mother at a car dealership in Holland. The dealer was insisting on a price. Mom remained calm, smiled, and pushed back with a counter-offer. He lowered his price slightly. She didn't flinch. They went back and forth like that, and I watched in awe as she calmly chipped away at the price.

I didn't fully understand the details, but I knew one thing—my mom wasn't going to settle. She wasn't intimidated by the salesman's persistence, and the longer they talked, the clearer it became that she was controlling the situation. By the end, she didn't get the price she initially wanted, but the deal was on her terms. In that moment, I learned that negotiation isn't just about winning a deal; it's about constantly adapting, reading the other person's reactions, and adjusting your approach to get closer to your goal. The business world isn't static, and if you don't adapt your strategies on the spot, you'll lose ground—fast.

> **In that moment, I learned that negotiation isn't just about winning a deal; it's about constantly adapting, reading the other person's reactions, and adjusting your approach to get closer to your goal.**

That lesson stuck with me more than any I'd been taught in school. There was no lecture, no textbook, no test; just me standing there, watching my mom make a deal in real time. Years later, when I found myself sitting across from bankers and investors, I would pull the techniques I learned from that moment, understanding that success isn't given but rather taken through persistence, control, and knowing your own value. Only real life can teach a lesson like that.

> **The business world isn't static, and if you don't adapt your strategies on the spot, you'll lose ground—fast.**

When I moved to Germany for university, the reality was different. In that country, who you are matters as much as what you know, and therefore, status can be everything. I didn't come from wealth, and being in a place that valued formality, structure, and social hierarchy put me at a disadvantage. I was also Middle Eastern, and no matter how much Germany claims to have evolved over the decades, it's still not as open toward strangers as other countries. I had the skill to close deals with the best of them, but without a title or a German passport, no one took me seriously. I could see it in the eyes of colleagues during meetings—to them, I was too young, too foreign, too inexperienced.

This was my first lesson in a contrarian truth: Success isn't just about what you know; it's about adapting to what others expect of you, even if that means playing by rules you don't agree with. In Germany, without the right title, I was as good as invisible, and I quickly realized that if I didn't adapt to these rules, I'd be pushed to the sidelines.

So, I did what I had to do—I earned my doctorate, not because I needed the education, but because I needed the validation. And, let me tell you, the moment I added "Dr." in front of my name, everything changed. Suddenly, banks started listening, older professionals returned my calls, and deals that once felt impossible were now within reach.

This choice may make me seem like a sellout. Most people pursue degrees for knowledge, not status. But here's a contrarian truth: Sometimes you need to play by the rules of the system you're in—even if it's just to earn the freedom to eventually break them. Adapting to cultural expectations can be a powerful way to control the narrative in your favor.

> **Sometimes you need to play by the rules of the system you're in—even if it's just to earn the freedom to eventually break them.**

The degree gave me credibility, but it didn't prepare me for the real challenges I faced in business. What my degree didn't teach me is that success in real life isn't formulaic. The theories you learn in school assume that things go according to plan, but life rarely works that way. Adapting in business means being ready for the unpredictable, learning on the go, and changing course quickly when things don't work out as planned. Those who adapt thrive; those who don't fall behind.

In school, you're taught theory—how things should work. But business doesn't follow neat formulas or predictable paths. Success depends on learning to adapt, pivot, and manage situations no textbook could ever cover. Besides, the classroom teaches you to avoid failure, but in business, failure is inevitable. And I believe the difference between those who succeed and those who don't lies in how each handles failure.

For example, before my investing took off, I was running a construction company that was scaling quickly—in fact, too quickly. Within six months, I had eighteen employees under my belt, business was booming, and I felt invincible. Everything seemed to be going exactly as planned. But then an argument broke out between some key employees—guys who had been there from the beginning. Before I knew it, one person walked, then another. The very foundation of the company began to crumble, and it happened faster than I could react. I was young, ambitious, and determined to grow, but I was naive. I didn't understand that relying too much on a single person or a small core team could be fatal. When those key people left, the entire operation came to a grinding halt. Without the right infrastructure or diversified risk, I was exposed. I had placed too much trust in too few people, and when things went wrong, it was catastrophic.

Suddenly, the thriving business I'd built from the ground up was on the verge of bankruptcy. I was scrambling to save what I could, but no amount of late-night phone calls or last-minute deals could reverse what was happening. The business collapsed, and I was left to pick up the pieces. It was a brutal lesson, but it cemented for me the truth that businesses, like people, must adapt or risk becoming obsolete. That failure was my wake-up call: If I wanted to succeed long term, I'd have to prepare to pivot, evolve, and survive the hard blows, not just chase growth.

Here's what I learned from that failure.

DIVERSIFY YOUR TALENT POOL

In today's world, relying on a single person or limited perspective isn't just risky—it's a path to obsolescence. If you fail to diversify your team, you're essentially betting your future on something that can disappear in a moment.

DON'T GROW TOO FAST

Scaling quickly without stability is a recipe for disaster. More than 70 percent of start-ups scale too quickly, focusing on growth without the right infrastructure.[2] Sustainable growth is what keeps a business alive. By growing too fast, I learned the hard way that adaptability matters far more than speed.

I had jumped too far ahead without building the right systems to support that growth. From then on, I focused on sustainable growth—building at a pace where I could handle setbacks and still keep moving forward. Rapid growth without stability is tempting, but it's short-sighted. You have to adapt in stages, making sure you're building on solid ground, or you risk losing everything you've built. Success should feel sustainable, not like you're running on a tightrope.

---

2   Max Marmer et al., "Startup Genome Report Extra on Premature Scaling," Startup Genome, last modified March 2012, https://startupgenome.com/reports/startup-genome-why-startups-fail-premature-scaling.

> **Success should feel sustainable, not like you're running on a tightrope.**

PREPARE FOR THE WORST

Every entrepreneur believes their business will succeed, but what happens when it doesn't? Failure is inevitable in some form or another; the key is to prepare for it. I hadn't put the right contingency plans in place, and it nearly destroyed me. These were hard-learned lessons, but they were lessons I never could have received from a textbook or a business seminar.

> **Failure is inevitable in some form or another; the key is to prepare for it.**

How to Get an A in Failure

When you're forced to adapt to unpredictable challenges, when the stakes are high, and when failure is a very real possibility, that's when real-life learning happens. That's why I believe the most successful entrepreneurs aren't necessarily the ones with the most degrees—they're the ones who know how to think on their feet.

So how do you know if you're a real-life learner? Ask yourself the following questions:

- When was the last time you took a risk, knowing failure was a possibility, but did it anyway?
- How often do you see uncertainty as a catalyst for growth, rather than a setback?

- What's one failure that forced you to pivot and ultimately led to your biggest breakthrough?

These questions don't just challenge you to think; they push you to adapt to failure. In today's world, change is constant, and the entrepreneurs who survive aren't the ones who get everything right—they're the ones who can adapt, learn, and pivot quickly when they're faced with setbacks. The reality is simple: If you can't adapt, you won't survive in business.

Real learning is messy. It happens when deals fall apart, when you have to fire people, when you have to figure out how to keep a business afloat in the face of disaster. It's when you make a call at 2:00 a.m. to save a deal or when you have to admit that you made a mistake and find a way to fix it.

> **The reality is simple: If you can't adapt, you won't survive in business.**

And sometimes you have to learn the same lesson twice. In 2016, a guy I knew came to me with a solid idea for a restaurant, and I decided to back him financially. He knew how to manage a company, and everything seemed to be going great. We brought in a talented head chef, and within three months, the restaurant was booming. But then the chef, seeing how much the success of the business hinged on him, said he wouldn't keep working there unless we increased his pay.

We gave in, not once, but two or three times. The problem was, we didn't have a backup plan and were at his mercy. Suddenly, we realized that while we were the business owners, it was the cook who really owned the business. At first, I didn't have the right contingency plan, but after my earlier experience with the construction company, I knew I had to adapt quickly, or I'd be repeating the same mistake. Adaptation wasn't just a choice; it was a necessity to survive in this business.

How did I handle it? Well, I had to change my strategy. We couldn't keep playing his game. I ended up closing the restaurant under the guise of a renovation. We actually did some minor remodeling to the space, but the real goal was to buy time to find new staff. This time, I hired two cooks, making sure we never found ourselves in that vulnerable position again. Lesson learned—twice!

Most people avoid failure. They fear it, shy away from it, and do everything they can to steer clear of it. But here's the truth that most successful entrepreneurs won't tell you: Failure isn't something to avoid; it's something to embrace. It forces you to adapt. Those who refuse to adapt after failure are the ones who fall behind, fade into obscurity, or go out of business. If you're not evolving, you're becoming obsolete. In business, if you're not adapting, you're already dead.

Take a moment to think about a failure you've experienced recently—whether in business, a personal project, or even a relationship. Think about it. That failure could hold the key to your next big breakthrough, but only if you're willing to adapt your approach. Ask yourself: "How can I change what didn't work? What new strategy can I apply to keep moving forward?" Every failure is an opportunity to adapt, improve, and eventually succeed. The failure is only final if you don't change your mindset, your strategy, or your actions.

Embrace failure as part of your education. It's a powerful teacher, if you're willing to listen. If you're afraid to fail, you'll never reach your full potential. You'll play it safe, avoid risks, and ultimately limit your growth. But if you can reframe failure as a critical part of your learning process, you'll be able to take bigger leaps, make smarter decisions, and recover faster when things don't go your way. As Reid

Hoffman, cofounder of LinkedIn, once said, "If you are not embarrassed by the first version of your product, you've launched too late."[3] It's about adapting quickly, learning from mistakes, and constantly iterating. That's the real key to success.

> **Every failure is an opportunity to adapt, improve, and eventually succeed. The failure is only final if you don't change your mindset, your strategy, or your actions.**

The Power of One Mentor

Everyone loves to talk about the power of networking these days. "Your network is your net worth," so the saying goes, and countless events are built around the idea that the more people you meet, the more successful you'll be. Don't get me wrong—networking is valuable. But the conventional belief that networking alone will get you to the top is a half-truth at best. If you want to accelerate your growth, you don't need a million contacts in your phone or a million followers in your feed; you just need one solid mentor.

A good mentor is your secret weapon because they cut through the noise and give you the straight, unfiltered truth. They give you focused, personalized guidance you simply won't get from a room full of business cards. Networking might open doors, but a mentor helps you walk through those doors with confidence and direction. The right mentor

---

[3] Reid Hoffman, *Blitzscaling: The Lightning-Fast Path to Building Massively Valuable Companies* (Crown Currency, 2018).

will challenge your thinking, push you beyond your limits, and help you avoid mistakes they've already made. They're like a cool uncle who is willing to show you the ropes after they've already fallen off them a hundred times. They fast-track your growth by sharing their experience—the lessons you would otherwise have to learn the hard way. But not all mentors are created equal.

> **Networking might open doors, but a mentor helps you walk through those doors with confidence and direction.**

How to Find the Right Mentor

In my twenties, I was driven, ambitious, and eager to break into the commercial real estate world. I attended every networking event I could find, shaking hands and collecting business cards like they were tickets to success. But even after meeting hundreds of people, I realized that I wasn't learning enough. Sure, I had connections, but those connections weren't turning into knowledge or pushing me to be better. I needed someone who could show me the ropes—someone who could go beyond small talk and give me real insights into the business, who felt as invested as I was in my success.

I went through a few false starts with potential mentors who, online, seemed like they'd be a perfect fit. They were successful and well connected and had the kind of experience I was after. But something was always off. Either they didn't have the time, or their values didn't align with mine. I didn't just want a teacher; I needed someone who shared my vision and understood where I wanted to go.

Then I met Manny. Manny was a heavy hitter in the commercial real estate world—older, battle-tested, and not afraid to tell it like it is. I first saw him as a guest on *Steve Harvey*. Then I started following him on social media platforms and reading about him in online articles until I finally reached out to him. He saw potential in me, but he didn't coddle me. Manny taught me that the real lessons don't come from easy answers; they come from hard questions. He pushed me to think critically, look at deals differently, and understand the bigger picture. Most importantly, Manny had values that aligned with mine. Like me, he'd built his empire from scratch. But also like me, he wasn't just in it for the money—he was in it to build something meaningful, something that would last. We connected because we both wanted the same things out of life and business: growth, impact, and legacy. That's why our mentorship worked.

To find the right mentor, you have to be intentional and strategic. Here are the steps I followed to help me find mentors like Manny who pushed me to the next level:

1. Identify someone in your niche who aligns with your goals.
   You want someone who understands the specific challenges of your industry.

   Ask yourself: Are they where you want to be in five or ten years? Do they think the way you aspire to think?

2. Be clear on what you want to learn and why they can help you.
   When you approach a mentor, you need to be specific about what you want to learn and why you think they're the right person to help you grow. Mentors are busy people, and if you come to them with vague requests, you'll get vague guidance.

   Ask yourself: How do my objectives align with their expertise?

3. Make sure they're willing to share.
   The key to getting the most out of a mentor is asking the right questions. Don't just ask for their opinions—ask them to share their failures, their lessons learned, and the turning points

in their career. This is where the gold is. And they should be generous with that gold.

Ask yourself: Do I feel taken into their confidence?

4. Evaluate whether your mentor is still the right fit.
As you grow, you may outgrow your mentor. And that's okay. The mentor who helped you in the early stages of your career might not be the one who helps you take things to the next level.

Ask yourself: Are you still learning from this person? Or is it time to seek new perspectives?

Mentorship is not a one-time transaction. It's a relationship that evolves as you do. When I first started working with Manny, he was exactly what I needed—someone to teach me the ropes, show me the inner workings of commercial real estate, and push me to think bigger. But as I grew, so did my needs. Manny's role in my life shifted from teacher to peer. That's when I knew it was time to expand my circle of mentors.

At some point, you'll need multiple mentors for different aspects of your life and career. One mentor might guide you through your business challenges, while another might help you develop personally or spiritually. The key is to recognize when you need to bring new people into your life who can challenge you in ways your current mentors can't.

Warning Signs: How to Spot a Bad Mentor

1. **All Talk, No Listen**
   Red Flag: They spend more time telling you about their accomplishments than listening to your challenges.

2. **The Disappearing Act**
   Red Flag: They're never around when you actually need advice, always too "busy" to mentor properly.
3. **Stuck in the Past**
   Red Flag: Their advice is outdated, based on experiences that don't align with modern business practices.
4. **Control Freak**
   Red Flag: They micromanage your decisions instead of helping you develop your own solutions.
5. **Cheerleader, Not Coach**
   Red Flag: They give you endless encouragement but offer little in the way of practical, actionable advice.

My Million-Dollar Wake-Up Call

Many believe that once you've achieved a certain level of success, you can finally take your foot off the gas and coast on your past accomplishments. But that's a dangerous mindset. The idea that you can ever truly "make it" is an illusion. In reality, mastery is never achieved. No matter how much you know, there's always something new to learn, something else to discover, and new skills to develop. The moment you stop learning is the moment you start to lose your edge.

Lifelong learning is a necessity if you're serious about being a top-tier entrepreneur. No matter how high you climb, there's always more work to be done, more knowledge to gain, and more skills to master. I learned this lesson the hard way, nearly losing a multimillion-dollar deal because I got too comfortable.

> **No matter how much you know, there's always something new to learn, something else to discover, and new skills to develop. The moment you stop learning is the moment you start to lose your edge.**

A few years into my career, I landed what felt like a dream deal. It was a multimillion-dollar real estate transaction, and all the pieces seemed to be falling into place. I negotiated well, put together a solid team, and was feeling on top of the world. But I let my guard down. I started to think, *I've got this. I've mastered this game.* That's when everything started to unravel.

What I didn't realize at the time was that I had started coasting. I had stopped pushing myself, and I had stopped learning. In the middle of the deal, I missed a critical detail in the contract. A competitor swooped in and leveraged that oversight to try to steal the deal right out from under me. By the time I realized what had happened, it was nearly too late. The situation became a crisis, and I scrambled to save the deal. I reached out to one of my mentors for advice, and he gave me a brutal wake-up call. "You got too comfortable," he told me. "You thought you'd made it, and you stopped paying attention. You're never done learning. Never."

Those words hit me like a ton of bricks. He was right. I had let my own success get to my head. I had assumed that because I had a few big wins under my belt, I could relax. But success isn't a finish line—it's a moving target. And if you're not constantly learning, constantly improving, you'll miss the target completely.

> **But success isn't a finish line—it's a moving target. And if you're not constantly learning, constantly improving, you'll miss the target completely.**

Mastery Is a Myth

Here's the truth most people don't want to hear: You never fully master anything. Sure, you can become highly skilled, highly knowledgeable, and incredibly successful. But the idea that you can reach a point at which you know it all and no longer need to grow is pure fantasy. The business world is constantly evolving, and if you're not evolving with it, you're falling behind. Whether it's new technologies, changing market trends, or shifts in consumer behavior, there's always something that can disrupt your business if you're not paying attention. And the only way to stay ahead is by continually learning.

Take a look at any top-tier entrepreneur, and you'll see a common thread: They never stop gaining new knowledge. They're always reading, attending seminars, listening to podcasts, or finding ways to challenge themselves. They don't view learning as something they did in the past; they view it as something that's woven into their everyday lives. And they're guarding themselves against the hidden enemy of growth that I'd almost let get the better of me: comfort. If you think you've learned all you need to learn, you're wrong. And if you think you can coast on your past achievements, you're going to get left behind.

> **The business world is constantly evolving, and if you're not evolving with it, you're falling behind.**

Lifelong learning happens when you stay hungry and recognize that no matter how far you've come, there's always further to go. There's always another skill to develop, another strategy to learn, and another challenge to tackle. Mastery is a myth, but growth is real, and it's ongoing.

> ## Commit to Learning Something New Every Week
>
> If you want to stay ahead in business and in life, you have to make learning a part of your daily routine. Commit to learning something new every week. It doesn't have to be earth-shattering or time-consuming, and it doesn't even have to directly relate to your business. It could be something as simple as reading a new book, watching a YouTube video, or attending a seminar. The key is to stay curious and open to new ideas.
>
> Here are some practical ways to integrate learning into your life:
>
> - Read a new book: Whether it's a business book, a biography, or even a novel, reading opens your mind to new perspectives and ideas.
> - Listen to a podcast: There are countless podcasts out there that can help you learn about everything from leadership to personal growth to market trends.
> - Attend a seminar or webinar: Sometimes hearing from an expert in your field can spark new ideas and challenge your current ways of thinking.
> - Try something outside your comfort zone: Take up a new hobby, try a new skill, or learn something outside your industry. The key is to keep pushing yourself to grow in unexpected ways.

> - Teach something you know: Often the best way to really get good at something is to teach it to someone else. It reinforces the basics and forces you to go deeper into the subject matter.
>
> The goal here is to challenge yourself and find ways to stretch your thinking and push the boundaries of what you know.

When was the last time you actively learned something new that challenged your beliefs? Take a moment to think about it. Have you been coasting, or are you constantly seeking new knowledge and perspectives? If it's been a while since you've felt truly challenged, it's time to shake things up. Find something that pushes you out of your comfort zone and forces you to think differently. For me, it was writing this book and growing my online presence. I have always been a private person, so to expose myself to the spotlight and put my intimate memories on the page was definitely a stretch for me at first. But it's been a growth opportunity that has been 100 percent worth it.

Steps to Keep Learning

Getting better at something is a lifelong process, and maintaining that edge requires deliberate effort. Growth doesn't happen by accident, and real learning isn't something I can leave behind after I've "made it." I have to keep seeking new perspectives, new challenges, and fresh voices to guide me.

One of the great discoveries I've made about learning is that it's cyclical. Ideally, every cycle should begin with a new mentor. When I was building my real estate portfolio, I sought guidance from someone with industry experience. I initially found Manny, a mentor with a similar background, who helped me navigate commercial real estate deals. But when I started scaling my portfolio, Manny's expertise, while invaluable, wasn't enough to help me raise capital or restructure large-scale investments. That's when I began searching for new mentors with the specific expertise I needed for the next stage in my career.

> **Ideally, every cycle should begin with a new mentor.**

By committing to finding a new mentor annually, I give myself the opportunity to gain fresh insights and stay sharp. This doesn't mean abandoning my previous mentors. Instead, I gather multiple viewpoints, increasing the diversity of thought that fuels my success.

Here's some advice: Once you've found a mentor, commit to at least three sessions with them. Why three? Because mentorship isn't something that happens in a single conversation. In the first meeting, you don't even know what you don't know. The second meeting allows you to go deeper, and by the third, you'll start to see patterns, lessons, and actionable steps emerge. These sessions give you a deeper understanding of your field and your mentor's approach to solving problems.

Besides finding a mentor, another key to staying ahead is engaging in fields outside your expertise. I've learned through experience that sticking too closely to my own lane limits my growth. Whether it's listening to someone in a completely different industry or learning a skill that doesn't seem immediately useful, expanding my horizons opens my mind to new ways of thinking.

Learning from different industries creates a toolbox of ideas that can be applied in unexpected ways. A few years ago, I found myself sitting at a table with a family who had built a legacy in the solar industry—the Krinners. Their business was based in Germany, but they had big plans that stretched beyond borders, aiming to expand their solar energy ventures to new territories. I had no experience in solar energy at all. My background was in real estate and commercial ventures, areas where I felt completely at home. But something about the Krinners' vision intrigued me, and I knew I had to listen.

It was during this meeting that the Krinners shared their bold plan to build a 7.5MW solar power plant outside of Germany. At that point, I had no idea how solar energy plants were built, what the logistics entailed, or how the financing would work. But what struck me most about this conversation was their deep commitment to sustainability and their clear sense of purpose. They weren't just in it for the profits—they genuinely believed in the potential of solar energy to change the world.

One thing I've learned in business is that often you have to adapt to succeed. And even though I had zero expertise in the solar industry, I saw an opportunity for growth. I wasn't going to let my lack of knowledge hold me back. I was open to learning, open to a new field, and, most importantly, open to being challenged.

The Krinners had built a strong family-run business, and their track record in solar projects spoke for itself. They had already delivered successful projects within Germany, but this new project was a much bigger leap. Their plan to build a 7.5MW solar plant required a lot more than just capital—it needed a strategic approach to land acquisition, construction logistics, and navigating the legal frameworks of a country outside Germany.

They asked for my help.

I knew it wasn't going to be easy. The solar industry was new to me, and the international scale of the project added a whole new layer of complexity. But instead of backing away, I embraced the challenge. I understood that the real value of this opportunity wasn't just in the project itself—it was in the learning that would come with it. If I could help the Krinners bring this vision to life, I would not only broaden my business expertise, but I would also grow personally and professionally in ways I hadn't anticipated.

My final advice for continuing to learn is this: Seek failure. (No, that's not a typo.) If you're not failing, you're not learning. My near-bankruptcy moment during the collapse of my construction company taught me more about resilience, contingency planning, and talent diversification than any success ever could. It's easy to get comfortable when things are going well, but real growth happens in failure. I learned that the hard way when key employees left, causing my company to fall apart. I was left scrambling to rebuild, but in the process, I became a stronger leader.

> **If you're not failing, you're not learning.**

By regularly taking calculated risks in my business, I open myself up to learning at a deeper level. I often remind people that it's not about gambling recklessly but about understanding that if you never fail, you're not taking big enough risks. This approach doesn't just make me more resilient—it gives me insights and teaches lessons that no textbook or success story ever could.

The final piece of this learning cycle is reflection. After I've gained new knowledge or gone through a failure, I need to pause and reflect. What did I learn from the experience? How can I apply it moving forward? Reflection turns failure into fuel for your next success. Without it, you risk repeating the same mistakes.

At the heart of lifelong learning is a relentless pursuit of growth. Be curious. Take risks. Seek knowledge. Whether you're embracing failure, finding new mentors, or engaging in industries outside your comfort zone, the key is to keep moving forward. Growth doesn't happen in a straight line—it's a cycle of learning, failing, and reflecting. Each step builds on the one before, creating a foundation that's unshakable.

> **At the heart of lifelong learning is a relentless pursuit of growth. Be curious. Take risks. Seek knowledge.**

Maverick Takeaways

- Success is temporary if you stop evolving; stagnation is a silent threat.
- Negotiation isn't just about winning; it's about setting terms on your own ground.
- Validation doesn't come from titles but from resilience and adaptability.
- Fast growth without structure leads to fragile success; build stability first.
- Real learning isn't in the classroom; it happens in real-life setbacks and mistakes.
- Dependency on a few people is a vulnerability; diversify talent to ensure resilience.
- Comfort is the enemy of progress; constant adaptation is your strongest asset.

CHAPTER NINE

The Power of No: Command Your Time, Dominate Your Life

Conventional thought: Saying no shuts down opportunities.

Maverick truth: Saying no allows you to prioritize.

Stop Being a Yes-Man

I'll never forget the moment I realized that saying yes to everything was killing my focus—and would eventually destroy the empire I was building. It was a Wednesday afternoon, and I was deep in negotiations for what could have been a landmark real estate deal. We were talking multimillion-dollar properties, contracts that could reshape my portfolio overnight. But as I sat there, phone in hand, something wasn't right. Instead of feeling excited, I felt a weight in my chest, this sense that I wasn't in control of my own time anymore.

In the middle of the meeting, my phone buzzed for the third time. Another offer. Another *opportunity*. I realized that I wasn't in command of my time—I was at the mercy of everyone else's agendas. That's when it hit me: My life had become a reaction to other people's priorities. Every time I said yes, I was pushing my own goals aside to make room for someone else's. And the truth was, this wasn't the first time it had happened. I'd been letting small, shiny distractions pull me off-track for months.

I ended the meeting, put my phone on airplane mode, and sat down at my desk. I grabbed a sheet of paper and started writing down every deal, every opportunity, every request that had come my way in the past month. I'd been saying yes to meetings that didn't move the needle, to projects that didn't align with my bigger vision. I was scattered, unfocused, and on the brink of losing what I'd worked so hard to build. That was the moment I knew something had to change. I had to start saying no—not just to bad deals, but to good ones, too, that just weren't right for me.

Ask yourself: Are you in control of your time, or are you letting other people hijack your schedule? Take a hard look at where your focus is going. How many of the things you're saying yes to are actually taking you closer to your goals?

When I first started practicing the art of saying no, it wasn't easy; there were many times when I felt like I was missing out. Turning down opportunities—especially ones that look good on the surface—comes with an inevitable pang of guilt. It feels like you're letting someone down or missing out on a what-if moment that could lead to something big. But here's the truth I had to learn: Saying no to one thing is saying yes to something better. Over time, I learned that my real power wasn't in endless expansion; it was in the precision to choose where my energy would make the most impact.

There was one deal in particular that tested me. It was a luxury real estate project—a sprawling commercial property in downtown Los Angeles. On paper, it was perfect. The numbers were solid, the potential was huge, and every part of me wanted to say yes. But something was off. It didn't align with where I wanted to go. The project would have required my time and energy for at least three years—time I knew I needed to invest in building out a new division of my company.

> **Saying no to one thing is saying yes to something better.**

I hesitated. I could feel the pull of the deal. My instinct was to grab it before someone else did. But I stopped. I reminded myself of what I'd written down that day in my office: *Focus on what matters, not what looks good on paper.* One of the key insights that helped me was defining what my success should look like five, even ten years down the line. I took time to create a clear vision for my business and my life. This meant setting concrete long-term goals and identifying the specific milestones that would get me there. I learned that, without a clear vision, it's easy to get lost in short-term wins and scattered decisions. By defining my big-picture goals, it became easier to identify when an opportunity aligned with my purpose—and when it didn't.

So, I said no. A month later when the property market in that area tanked, I was so glad I did. The deal would have turned into a hot mess, draining my resources and pulling me offtrack. By saying no, I dodged a bullet—and more importantly, I stayed focused on what mattered. That decision allowed me to scale my business in the way I'd originally envisioned, without distractions.

Take a minute today to write down your top three long-term goals. For each opportunity that comes your way, ask yourself: Does this bring me closer to one of those goals? If not, be bold and say no. Protect your time like it's your most valuable asset—because it is.

Once I got comfortable with saying no, I saw how much freedom it gave me—not just in business, but in every area of my life. My time was my own again. I wasn't running around putting out fires and chasing opportunities that didn't serve me. I could now focus on the projects and people that aligned with my long-term vision. Sometimes I had to let go of relationships, friendships, and even family expectations. I lost people along the way, people who couldn't understand why I wasn't the yes guy anymore. But you know what? The people who stuck around respected me more for it. And the ones who didn't? Well, they weren't aligned with where I was going anyway.

Conventional thought believes that saying no will close doors and limit your opportunities. But I'm living proof that saying no actually keeps the right doors open—the ones that truly matter. Think about your own life: How many of the opportunities you're saying yes to are really just distractions? What would happen if you started saying no more often? Whom or what would you lose—and whom or what would you gain?

Time Is Your Weapon; Guard It Like a Beast

In the world of empire building, there's one weapon you can't afford to wield carelessly: time. Every second that slips through your fingers is a second someone else uses to get ahead. For me, time wasn't just an asset—it was my greatest strategic advantage. But to wield it effectively, I had to guard it with unrelenting focus, like my future depended on it—because it did.

> **In the world of empire building, there's one weapon you can't afford to wield carelessly: time. Every second that slips through your fingers is a second someone else uses to get ahead.**

When I first started out, I thought hustling meant saying yes to everything. Every deal, every meeting, every opportunity—if it showed up on my radar, I took it. I figured the more I had on my plate, the more successful I'd become. But the reality was, I was spreading myself too thin. Instead of dominating the deals that mattered, I was getting bogged down by distractions. My time was being drained, and I had no idea how much damage it was causing until I hit my breaking point.

One day, I looked at my calendar and realized that out of two dozen meetings I'd scheduled that month, only five of them had pushed my goals forward. The rest had been complete time wasters. That's when I decided to stop playing defense and start playing offense with my time.

Here are the principles I came up with and still live by today:

- Narrow down your core focus: Before you can guard your time, you need to know what deserves your attention. Write down the three core areas of your business or life that move the needle. These are your nonnegotiables. For me, it was real estate strategy, scaling my portfolio, and developing high-impact relationships. If a meeting or task didn't support one of these, it didn't make it onto my calendar.

- Say no to distractions early and often: The faster you can say no, the more time you save. Start every week by reviewing your schedule. Ask yourself, "What on this list can I say no to right now?" Clear the distractions before they even hit your desk. This exercise can be a lot of fun, like playing a video game where you eliminate the enemy time snatchers.

- Create a fortress of time blocks: Protecting your time means creating strict boundaries for when and how you work. Block out specific chunks of time each day for deep, focused work. No distractions, no meetings, no interruptions. Every day, I block out two hours of uninterrupted work time. No calls, no emails—just high-level strategy and execution. This is where the real growth happens.

- Automate your no: Saying no yourself, every time, takes time. Use tools such as autoresponders or human assistants to handle basic requests and turn down low-priority meetings automatically. I trained my assistant to handle all inbound meeting requests. If something wasn't mission-critical, she declined it without even bothering me. The result? I freed up my calendar and energy to focus on what mattered.

- Evaluate every opportunity against your goals: Not every prospect is worth pursuing, even if it looks good on paper. Before committing to anything, ask yourself, "Does this serve my long-term goals?" If the answer is no, then you know what to do.

How many of the items on your schedule this week are truly moving you closer to your goals? If they aren't, why are you still saying yes to them? Imagine your future self one year from now. If you could only invest in three projects or commitments this year, what would your future self have wanted them to be? How much of your current schedule would you actually keep?

Drop the Hammer: Say No and Mean It

Once, I was sitting in a meeting across from one of the biggest investors in Munich. We'd been working together for years, and this guy had a knack for bringing in deals that turned heads. So when he came to me with what he described as a "no-brainer opportunity," I should've jumped at it. That's what he thought, anyway.

The deal was flashy, big, and promising insane returns. But there was one problem—it didn't fit my strategy. My gut told me no, but saying no out loud wasn't going to be easy. I respected this guy, and we'd made a lot of money together. Turning him down felt like turning my back on an ally. But here's the thing: When you're building an empire, you don't let relationships or pressure cloud your judgment. If it's not right, it's not right. So I said no.

What happened next shocked me. Instead of getting upset, he nodded. "I respect that," he said. "You've always had a clear vision for where you're going." That's when I realized that saying no doesn't just protect your time and focus; it builds respect. People appreciate when you know exactly what you want—and when you have the guts to turn down opportunities that don't align with that. Judging from his response, this business guy most likely has the same practice of saying no, which explains his own wild success.

But besides learning to say no, you have to learn to say it in the right way. Otherwise, you'll burn bridges and lose other opportunities.

> **People appreciate when you know exactly what you want—and when you have the guts to turn down opportunities that don't align with that.**

Five Ways to Say No Artfully

If you're going to master the art of saying no, you need a playbook. Here are five ways I've learned to say no without burning bridges—and how you can use them to protect your empire:

1. The Gratitude No

   Acknowledge the offer and thank the person for thinking of you. Then explain why you're passing. People like to feel appreciated. Even when you're turning them down, they'll respect that you value their offer. When I turned down that big investor, I didn't just say no and walk away. I made sure he knew I appreciated the opportunity. That small gesture kept our relationship strong, and a few months later, he brought me another deal—one that fit perfectly with my vision.

   Sample script: *Thanks so much for thinking of me for this opportunity. I really appreciate it. Right now, though, I'm focused on [X], and I need to stay committed to that. I'm sure this will be a great success for you, though!*

2. The Redirect No

   Say no, but offer a helpful alternative. This way, you're still adding value without committing your time. People appreciate solutions.

   Sample script: *This sounds like a great project, but I'm unable to commit right now. Have you thought about reaching out to [Name]? I think they'd be a great fit for this.*

3. The Soft No with a Future Option

   Let them know you're interested, but the timing isn't right. Keep the door open for future collaboration.

   Sample script: *This sounds like a great opportunity, but my plate is full right now. Let's revisit this in a few months when my schedule frees up.*

4. The Priorities No
   Be up front and clear about your current priorities. Explain why the offer doesn't fit into your current focus. People respect someone who is focused and intentional.

   Sample script: *Right now, I'm laser focused on [X priority], and I have to be really selective about what I take on. This project doesn't fit into that vision, but I'm rooting for your success!*

5. The "No for Now" with a Contingency
   Let the person know that while you can't commit now, you're willing to reconsider if the circumstances change—but with clear boundaries. This keeps the conversation open and ups the chance that the next time they present an offer, it will be more in your favor.

   Sample script: *I'm not able to commit to this right now, but if you can adjust the timeline or scope, I'd be open to discussing it again. Let me know if that's an option.*

The key is learning how to say it without damaging relationships or losing respect. Think of the last three opportunities you said yes to that didn't serve your goals. How could you have said no more effectively? What kind of no would've protected your time without burning bridges?

Protect Your Energy: Don't Waste It on the Small Stuff

I'll be honest—there was a time in my late twenties when I was all about the money. If it looked good on paper, I'd jump at it. So, when a flashy side project came my way, offering easy money and minimal effort, I couldn't resist. I told myself it wouldn't take much time and that I could handle it without losing focus on my real estate empire. But what I didn't realize was that time wasn't the issue—energy was.

From the moment I agreed to the project, I felt my energy draining. It wasn't just about the hours I spent on it, though those added up quickly enough. It was the constant mental strain—the nagging thoughts about it that followed me everywhere, pulling my focus away from what mattered most. My creativity started to dip. I felt sluggish, and, worst of all, my drive for my core business began to fade.

After a few months of pushing through, I had to make a tough call. I walked away from the project, leaving money on the table. But what I gained was worth so much more: my energy, my focus, and my momentum.

Energy Audit Exercise

Take the time to go through this exercise and dig deep. You'll be amazed at how much clarity it brings.

STEP 1: IDENTIFY YOUR HIGH-ENERGY WORK

You know those moments when you are fully dialed in and walk out of a meeting or finish a task feeling like you've just moved mountains? That's high-energy work—activities that not only fuel your focus but also leave you energized and motivated, like a great workout.

Think back over the last month. What work gave you that kind of energy? What tasks or projects left you feeling sharper and more creative? Write down three to five examples of high-energy work. Look for common threads. What made these tasks different from the ones that drained you? Was it the type of project? The people involved? The impact it had on your larger goals?

For me, it's always the big-picture work that gets me charged: strategy meetings, vision casting, high-stakes negotiations. For my wife, it's the more detail-oriented tasks related to our business that fuel her. That's why we make such a good team.

STEP 2: FIND YOUR ENERGY VAMPIRES

Now it's time to get real. We all have those tasks or commitments that suck the life out of us. Whether it's that client, tenant, friend, or relative who always needs "one more thing" or the endless stream of emails, these are your energy vampires. What tasks, projects, or people consistently drain your energy? Be brutally honest with yourself. What commitments do you walk away from feeling depleted instead of energized? List the top three energy vampires in your life right now. This is the first step to cutting them out or finding a way to minimize their impact on your day-to-day energy levels.

My cousin Omid was one of my closest friends growing up, so when he asked for a little advice on getting his small business up and running, I didn't hesitate. But soon, "a little advice" turned into weekly sessions, where he'd want feedback on his website, help with his marketing plan, or just someone to brainstorm ideas with. Omid meant well, but every time I saw his number pop up, I knew my evening was about to get hijacked. One day, after a three-hour call that ate up my entire Sunday afternoon, I realized I had to draw a line. I let him know that while I wanted to see him succeed, I couldn't keep dedicating hours of my time each week to his business. I suggested he look into hiring a business coach or joining an entrepreneur group. It was a tough conversation, but he understood. We're still close, and now, instead of dreading his calls, I actually look forward to our catch-ups—minus the endless "business help."

STEP 3: MAP YOUR ENERGY PEAKS AND LOWS

Energy is time sensitive. We all have times during the day when we're at our sharpest and times when we're just going through the motions. Mapping out these peaks and valleys is critical to understanding how to maximize your energy.

Over the next three days, track your energy levels. When do you feel most focused, creative, and motivated? When do you hit a slump? Write down your observations. Are you most energized in the mornings? Does your energy dip after lunch? By mapping your energy, you'll know exactly when to schedule your high-energy work and when to tackle the low-priority tasks.

For me, early mornings, while most people are still sleeping, are always my golden time. That's when I tackle the hardest, most critical thinking work. Afternoons? Those are for meetings, admin, and anything that doesn't require my full creative energy.

STEP 4: ELIMINATE THE ENERGY DRAINS

This is where the rubber meets the road. Look back at the energy vampires you listed. What can you eliminate, delegate, or minimize? Are there tasks you can automate or hand off to someone else? Choose one energy vampire to eliminate this week. Make a concrete plan to either cut it out completely or significantly reduce its impact on your day-to-day energy.

The first on my hit list was David, my high-maintenance client who'd become notorious for after-hours calls and nonstop demands. One week, I decided to make a concrete plan to minimize his impact. I sent David a polite email, suggesting we simplify our communications to a weekly summary email and a single weekly call to go over any questions he might have.

To my surprise, David was on board. I crafted a clear, bullet-pointed agenda for our weekly calls, so there'd be no room for digressions or last-minute requests. By limiting my direct engagement, I reclaimed hours of focused work time each week—time I could now use to concentrate on bigger goals.

STEP 5: RECLAIM YOUR ENERGY RITUALS

Successful people understand the importance of rituals that bring their energy back to full capacity. Whether it's a workout, meditation, or a few minutes of creative downtime, these rituals are nonnegotiable. What activities help you recharge your energy? Think about moments when you've felt revitalized, even after a long day. These are your energy rituals.

> **Successful people understand the importance of rituals that bring their energy back to full capacity.**

(Note: Believe it or not, watching TV or YouTube can be an energy drain, even though it may feel invigorating in the moment. It can also lower your concentration levels over time. So make sure you limit your screen time.)

Commit to one energy ritual every day. It doesn't have to be long—whether it's a twenty-minute walk, a quick meditation session, or a series of squats or lifts, schedule it into your day as you would an important meeting. I make working out a daily ritual. No matter how packed my day is, I always carve out time to hit the gym to make sure I get my energy back.

Energy Mastery: Own Your Day, Own Your Success

Once you master your energy, trust me, you'll notice a difference. You'll be sharper, more focused, and more in control. When I finally made energy protection a priority, everything shifted. I started doing better work, and my creativity, drive, and focus were all dialed in. I also felt surprisingly free.

By *free*, I don't mean doing whatever you want; I mean having the control to focus on what truly matters, without distractions pulling you off course. It means owning your time and your priorities. Most people are reacting to other people's agendas, getting caught up in commitments that don't serve them. They say yes because they think they're being productive, but in reality, they're giving their time away to things that don't move them forward.

Some people also say yes because, for them, being agreeable is a priority. A contrarian doesn't bother with *agreeable*. I can't tell you how many times I've turned down a deal or a project and made a lot of people disappointed or even angry. I've learned over the years that getting a negative reaction from someone can sometimes be the clearest sign that I'm prioritizing my long-term goals and staying on track to building my empire. (I call it the frowny-face gauge.)

As you begin to master the art of saying no, protecting your time and energy becomes second nature. But the journey doesn't end there. In the entrepreneurial world, setbacks and failures are inevitable, and how you handle them will define the resilience and longevity of your success.

Maverick Takeaways

- Saying no to distractions enables true focus on what drives growth.
- Turning down a good opportunity preserves time for a great one.
- A strong no is a statement of priorities, not just rejection.
- No is a powerful boundary that protects your time and energy.
- Respected leaders say no often, knowing it builds credibility and trust.
- Effective use of no enhances productivity and reduces burnout.
- By guarding time with no, you create space for intentional, meaningful work.

CHAPTER TEN

Fail Fast, Learn Faster

Conventional thought:
Failure is not an option.

Maverick truth:
Failure is an opportunity.

When I first got into business, I had that typical "failure is not an option" mindset. Like many young entrepreneurs, I was influenced by movies such as *The Wolf of Wall Street*, where ambition and success seem limitless, and failure is something only the weak consider. Like so many others, I didn't pay attention to the catastrophic endings to those stories. I overlooked the main characters' unlearned lessons, their inevitable self-destruction, and their ultimate moral demise.

Looking back now, I see that failure is one of the most powerful tools we have to grow. Across my career, I've owned nine different businesses, yet only one of them truly succeeded. Why am I okay with this statistic? Because I learned to fail forward. Each attempt we make in building our empires, whether it works or crashes, brings value if you take the time to learn from it. Every misstep became part of my foundation, helping me to refine my approach for the next venture.

I've already talked about Barcode, the nightclub I opened in Germany. At the time, it seemed like a surefire path to quick cash—a business in a buzzing industry, with people eager to spend on entertainment and drinks. The rooms were packed, the money was steady, and I thought I'd hit the jackpot. But after a while, I realized I was just chasing trends, trying to keep up with what was popular, without any real foundation. A nightclub might make money in the short term, but it doesn't build a legacy. It's temporary, shallow, and dependent on an audience that can disappear overnight. That experience taught me a truth I hold to this day: Fast money is rarely lasting money.

> **Each attempt we make in building our empires, whether it works or crashes, brings value if you take the time to learn from it.**

Instead of breaking me, failure clarified my goals. I didn't want to chase the next big thing; I wanted to build something real, something that wouldn't fade with the latest trend. From that point on, I began to view failure differently—not as an ending, but as the beginning of deeper understanding and growth.

Jack Ma, the founder of Alibaba, gives entrepreneurs this advice: In your twenties, try as many things as possible; in your thirties, focus on the one thing you're passionate about; and in your forties, build it to last.[4] This idea—that the early years are meant for experimentation and

---

4   Kate Whiting, "3 of Jack Ma's Best Pieces of Advice," World Economic Forum, September 10, 2019, https://www.weforum.org/stories/2019/09/3-of-jack-ma-s-best-pieces-of-advice.

learning—is something I fully embrace, even if it means failing more often than succeeding.

Fast money is rarely lasting money.

By the time I founded my real estate company, I had poured every failure, every lesson into it. And even now, I tell people that if success is a journey from Level 1 to Level 10, I'm only at Level 2. Some people might reach Level 10 by owning a few properties or hitting a financial milestone, but for me, Level 10 is building a sustainable legacy. And I'm just getting started.

Young entrepreneurs often rush to start companies with the belief that they'll succeed right away. But the truth is, there's no perfect blueprint. You have to take chances, face setbacks, and keep adapting. If you look at failure as part of the journey, you can build something real, something that lasts.

The Art of Failing Forward: Turning Setbacks into Success

Think of turbulence on a plane—it's unsettling, yes, but no plane has ever crashed because of turbulence alone. Planes fall only when critical systems fail, not because of a rough ride.

One of my early ventures was a tech project I was certain would succeed. I had meticulously assembled a talented team, secured strong investments, and developed a comprehensive plan. Everything appeared to be aligned, each piece of the puzzle seemingly in its place. But despite all our best efforts, the venture simply couldn't gain traction. It was a humbling experience, a stark reminder that even the most carefully laid plans can come undone. And sometimes, it's not even about a flaw in the plan or a gap in execution; sometimes, the market isn't ready, or the timing just isn't right. This is why learning to detach emotionally from failure is essential in business. When you're invested in a project, it's easy to take failure personally, to see it as a reflection of your abilities or worth. Just because you give up on an idea doesn't mean you are giving up on yourself.

Think of failure like a mentor who doesn't sugarcoat feedback. It's the brutal coach who keeps your vision sharp and your focus on what truly matters. Instead of treating failure as a detour, see it as the training ground where you forge the skill of critical self-assessment. Look back at each setback and pull out at least three actionable lessons that can guide your next steps. This isn't about reliving defeat; it's about reprogramming your approach to risk, learning how to spot early indicators of trouble, and developing the confidence to pivot when the road isn't leading you where you need to go. The more you fail forward, the faster you become at recognizing the moves that work versus those that don't. It's no longer just a lesson in resilience but a strategy for achieving unstoppable momentum.

Over time, I learned that resilience is forged in setbacks. Each setback, each seemingly insurmountable obstacle, added another layer of resilience to my foundation, creating a base that was solid enough to support the weight of future success. It's like building muscle: Every repetition, every challenge you overcome, strengthens you, preparing you for the greater hurdles that lie ahead.

When things get tough, I always revisit my foundations. I ask myself why I started this journey in the first place. Reflecting on that original vision reminds me of everything I've sacrificed along the way—family, friends, sleep, money—all in the pursuit of my goal. By the time you're in this deep, there's no turning back. It's like being on a plane that's already mid-flight: The door is closed, the destination is set, and there's no getting off now. You have to see it through, turbulence and all.

For every young entrepreneur facing a tough break, remember that failure can be your greatest asset. Don't let it paralyze you or convince you to stop. Instead, see it as the turbulence that tests your wings and makes them stronger. Embrace each setback, absorb the lessons it brings, and move forward with renewed clarity and courage.

Why Quick Wins Don't Build Empires

There's a thrill in launching a new venture, especially when it feels like success is right around the corner. But after a few experiences with businesses that made quick money yet lacked substance, I began to see a pattern: Fast cash doesn't build something meaningful. If the goal is to leave a legacy, then it's essential to look beyond immediate wins.

> **If the goal is to leave a legacy, then it's essential to look beyond immediate wins.**

After the nightclub, I launched a marketing agency, looking for something that would stand the test of time. I was ready to invest in an idea with staying power, to build something more substantial. Yet, again, I found myself facing challenges. Competing with other agencies, struggling to stand out, pushing hard to create our space in the market—it all felt like the same chase in a different arena.

The agency ultimately didn't make it, but it left me with insights that have been invaluable ever since. For one, I learned that just because an idea sounds good or feels substantial doesn't mean it aligns with your strengths. The nightclub and agency ventures had potential, but they weren't the right fit for what I wanted to create. With each experience, I learned to ask myself: "Is this really the legacy I want to build? Does this align with what I believe in?" Learning to measure ventures not just by their profit potential but also by their alignment with a bigger vision has been one of the most important shifts in my thinking.

> **Fast money might satisfy the immediate goal, but if the foundation isn't built on purpose, it will always feel empty.**

This lesson goes beyond business mechanics; it's about the mindset of a lasting legacy. Fast money might satisfy the immediate goal, but if the foundation isn't built on purpose, it will always feel empty. When you pour energy into something, it has to be something you believe in, something you can see contributing to a future you're proud of. Building for the long run means prioritizing depth over speed, resilience over flash. This is the difference between building a monument and writing your name in the sand. A monument lasts, even when you're gone. Sand washes away, erasing all traces with the first wave. Real legacy requires more than short-term wins; it demands a foundation strong enough to endure beyond you. This isn't about building something that outlasts your lifetime just for the sake of it. It's about creating a footprint so deeply carved that it becomes a guiding path for others. Take stock of your pursuits, not just for how profitable they might seem today but for the values, ideas, and inspiration they'll bring to others in years to come. True entrepreneurs aren't just aiming to make a mark—they're looking to create a map for those who'll come next.

> **Building for the long run means prioritizing depth over speed, resilience over flash.**

Every venture I started taught me to fail fast and learn faster. The key was shifting my mindset: Instead of clinging to a vision that wasn't working, I began seeing failure as an opportunity to evolve. By failing fast, I refined my methods, defined my limits, and sharpened the instincts that would carry me through future endeavors. Each business I launched turned into a cycle of testing, learning, and adapting—skills that now shape everything I do.

> **True entrepreneurs aren't just aiming to make a mark—they're looking to create a map for those who'll come next.**

Traction Tracker Challenge

One of the most valuable lessons I learned was to track real metrics—not hopes, not assumptions, but hard data. Consider the opportunity costs of holding on to ideas that aren't working, and always have an exit plan before you even start. Define clear benchmarks and timelines. For instance, I would set a target revenue or milestone to hit within a year. If I couldn't reach that, it was time to reassess and, if necessary, step away. Holding on to something purely out of hope can drain your resources and derail your long-term vision.

This exercise is designed to give you a fresh, practical way to track your business traction and make smart pivots when needed.

HOW IT WORKS

1. Set your metrics.
   Start by identifying three to five key metrics that matter most for your business's success. These should be measurable and specific, such as monthly revenue, customer retention rate, engagement rate, or product feedback score. Avoid vague goals like "get more sales"—instead, aim for specific numbers or percentages that define traction for you.

2. Evaluate your data against your benchmarks.
   Ask yourself:
   - Have I reached my target for this metric?
   - What are the trends over the last three months?
   - If it's underperforming, why? Are there external factors, strategy gaps, or unexpected shifts?
   - What specific steps can I take to improve this metric next month?

3. Reset the targets.
   Based on your findings, make a small tweak to your target for the selected metric. Set a realistic improvement goal to keep the momentum going. By continuously refining your targets, you're keeping traction in real time and pivoting as needed.

4. Celebrate small wins.
   Treat yourself to a coffee break, a team shout-out, or even a social media post to acknowledge the progress you've made.

5. Reflect quarterly.
   To avoid getting caught up in the day-to-day grind, set aside time every three months to reflect on your progress. During this quarterly check-in, revisit your initial mission and vision. Are

you still on course? Have the small wins added up to measurable growth in the areas that matter most?

Bonus tip: Invite a few fellow entrepreneurs to participate and share monthly outcomes for accountability and shared learning.

Every legendary entrepreneur, every game-changing leader, has faced failure not just once but repeatedly. They didn't reach their heights by luck or shortcuts; they got there by seeing every setback as a piece of a larger puzzle. When you face setbacks, remember this: Each one is part of a unique playbook you're writing. No two journeys are the same, but every journey worth taking demands grit, purpose, and vision. Success is not just the summit; it's the steady climb, built with every lesson learned, every challenge faced, and every failure transformed into fuel. Keep your eyes on the legacy you're building, even when the path isn't clear, and you'll find that each step, even the stumbles, is leading you exactly where you're meant to go.

> **Keep your eyes on the legacy you're building, even when the path isn't clear, and you'll find that each step, even the stumbles, is leading you exactly where you're meant to go.**

Pivot or Quit

In the world of business and entrepreneurship, the landscape changes quickly. The ability to adjust, move with the market, or even change direction entirely is what keeps you resilient. A failed project is often just a sign that a pivot is needed—that there's a better way to reach your destination or that a new path might be worth exploring. This flexibility doesn't weaken your commitment; it strengthens it, making you more versatile and capable of navigating uncertainty.

Pivoting also requires a level of self-awareness that doesn't always come naturally. By asking yourself tough questions, assessing what's working and what isn't, and then having the courage to make a change, you'll be able to spin around a lot more quickly than you think. Accept the idea that every project has a life cycle and knowing when to transition is part of staying true to your vision. There's wisdom in knowing when to move on, when to channel your resources into something with greater potential, and when to let a venture run its course.

Knowing when to pivot and when to walk away is an important skill.

Recognizing when to pivot or quit is like fine-tuning an instrument to stay in harmony with the world's constantly changing rhythms. Sometimes, you'll need to switch gears when external forces—market shifts, new competitors, changing customer expectations—render your current path ineffective. Other times, the signals are internal, like diminishing passion or an imbalance between the effort and reward. In either case, stepping away isn't an admission of defeat; it's a strategic maneuver. Your mission isn't to hang on indefinitely but to build something meaningful and lasting. So don't just hold on—adapt, evolve, and be willing to reinvent yourself as often as it takes to stay true to your highest goals.

Knowing when to pivot and when to walk away is an important skill. Many entrepreneurs hold on longer than they should, watching resources drain away simply because they're too invested in their great idea or seeing their profits grow to see that a quick exit would have saved them far more in the long run. That's why before hitting rock bottom, you need to have a solid exit plan.

Early on, I used to believe that sticking with something, no matter how tough it got, was the key to success. But over time, I realized that persistence only works if you're on the right path. Knowing when to pivot isn't quitting; it's a skill, a strategic move that protects your resources and keeps you aligned with your ultimate goals. At the same time, staying in a sinking venture just because you're invested can do more harm than good. Walking away from a floundering business frees up your time and energy to focus on something more meaningful.

> **Knowing when to pivot isn't quitting; it's a skill, a strategic move that protects your resources and keeps you aligned with your ultimate goals.**

In any venture, plan for both the ascent and the exit. Give yourself a timeline—six, twelve, or even twenty-four months—to assess whether you're gaining the traction you need. Listen to feedback, adjust, and improve, but also know when it's time to let go.

The Pivot Perspective Exercise

To truly embrace the pivot mindset, here's a hands-on exercise designed to help you evaluate when it's time to shift gears—and turn those insights into actionable steps.

continued

The Pivot Perspective Exercise

Step 1: Assess the landscape.

Grab a notebook or open a document, and create two columns. Label one column *What's Working* and the other *What's Not Working*.

- Write down everything about your current venture or project, both positive and negative.
- Be brutally honest. List anything that feels off, isn't progressing, or drains your energy. Then, in the *What's Working* column, list everything that still excites you, produces results, or aligns with your ultimate vision.

Step 2: Perform a root cause analysis.

Take each point from the *What's Not Working* list and dig deeper.

- Next to each item, write down why it isn't working. Ask yourself: "Is this something I can improve? Is it tied to my own strengths or weaknesses? Is this issue something I'm passionate enough about to fix?"
- Get specific. The goal is to understand if these challenges are temporary or if they signal a deeper misalignment.

Step 3: Find the pivot points.

Using your "root cause" notes, identify which of these challenges could be solved with a pivot rather than persistence.

- For each item, ask yourself, "What would it look like if I pivoted here?"
- Consider a shift in approach, audience, or focus. Jot down potential changes and how they might solve the issue or align more closely with your goals.
- Run a "pivot simulation." Before making your decision, sketch out two or three scenarios that could arise from different pivot options. For each, outline the key steps you would take, the

resources you'd need, and any potential obstacles. Imagine the impacts, positive and negative, that these shifts could have on your day-to-day operations, cash flow, and goals.

Step 4: Visualize the future.
Take a moment to imagine your life post-pivot.

- Close your eyes and visualize a version of this project that addresses your *What's Working* list while eliminating the most significant *What's Not Working* issues.
- How does it feel? Are you more energized? Excited? Fulfilled?

Step 5: Make a decision.
Reflect on your findings.

- Decide if a pivot could enhance your success and longevity.
- If yes, define the first action you need to take to begin that pivot—whether it's researching a new market, scaling back, or seeking feedback from trusted advisors.

This exercise will help you approach your business decisions with clarity and build the flexibility you need to make pivots confidently. Remember, pivoting isn't giving up; it's positioning yourself for greater success.

Don't Be Chicken

One of the stories that's stuck with me through my toughest moments is that of Colonel Harland Sanders—the man behind KFC. When people think of KFC, they think of fried chicken and that famous red-and-white bucket, but when I look at KFC, I see something else entirely: I see resilience, grit, and a reminder that it's never too late to make your mark.

Sanders was sixty-two when he finally got his business going. Sixty-two! Most people would call it quits by then, especially after his fried chicken recipe had been rejected by more than one thousand people. He went door-to-door pitching his dream, hearing no after no, and yet he kept going. Before he made it, he was cooking chicken in gas stations, living out of his car, and making tweaks as he went along. By all counts, he looked like an aging loser. But in fact, he was winning much more than any younger businessperson who was resting on their laurels and avoiding risks.[5]

> **That's the essence of a true entrepreneur: a relentless drive to innovate, adapt, and pursue a vision no matter how long it takes.**

Every no he faced was a reminder of his vision, pushing him closer to his final yes. Sanders's journey shows us that persistence alone isn't enough—it's the willingness to learn, adjust, and keep going that eventually led him to success. He wasn't just creating a business; he was laying the foundation for a legacy, one door knock at a time. His resilience wasn't about clinging to a single idea but having the courage to improve it, over and over. And that's the essence of a true entrepreneur: a relentless drive to innovate, adapt, and pursue a vision no matter how long it takes.

So what do you do when the challenges come? You adapt. You don't wait. And you trust your instincts. We get gut feelings for a reason. In fact, recent science argues that the stomach is actually the first so-called brain—that is, the emotional and intuitive center of all people. That's why when danger is imminent, some people start to feel queasy or even

---

5 "The KFC Colonel Sanders Story," KFC, accessed February 28, 2025, https://www.kfc.ie/colonels-story.

vomit. I can't count how many times I've made decisions I might not have been able to explain logically with my mind but that I knew were right based on a tingling in my skin or a sensation in my gut.

But intuition on its own isn't enough—it has to be paired with strategy. As I learned from my early ventures, instinct can guide you to take risks and pivot when necessary, but strategic thinking ensures those risks are calculated and productive. Developing this balance between gut feeling and grounded planning has been one of the most valuable skills in my journey as an entrepreneur.

> **Instinct can guide you to take risks and pivot when necessary, but strategic thinking ensures those risks are calculated and productive.**

In my first businesses, I would sometimes push through that nagging feeling that something was off, convincing myself that with enough effort, everything would work out. Over time, I learned to listen to those subtle signals and then back them up with analysis, research, and planning. When I sensed that a project wasn't aligned with my vision, I learned to take a step back and ask why. Ignoring that instinct only led to wasted time and resources.

Balancing instinct with strategy starts with knowing yourself and understanding your strengths. If your instinct is telling you that something isn't right, it's often because your experience and knowledge are picking up on red flags before you consciously notice them. Harnessing that instinct means allowing it to inform your strategy but not letting it drive your decisions blindly.

That's where "intelligent intuition" comes into play. Intelligent intuition is the blend of experience, instinct, and actionable insights gathered from feedback, data, and honest self-assessment. For instance, if your instinct is warning you about a red flag, combine it with data to weigh your options strategically. This way, even if your gut feeling leads you to take a risk, it's a risk informed by analysis. Cultivating this balance means you're not just "going with your gut" but navigating with a powerful mix of intuition and foresight that can only come from combining experience and evidence.

Intelligent intuition is the blend of experience, instinct, and actionable insights gathered from feedback, data, and honest self-assessment.

For instance, before making a pivot, I make it a point to run my instinctive reactions through this checklist of questions:

- ☐ Is this direction sustainable?
- ☐ Does it align with my long-term goals?
- ☐ What evidence supports or contradicts my instinct?

Next, I look out for red flags. Here are some of the biggest ones to pay attention to:

- × **Stagnant or declining metrics**
  When data show a steady drop or when growth flatlines over months, that's my cue to dig deeper.
- × **Overextended resources with no return**
  I can't count the times I've invested heavily in staff, marketing, or resources, thinking this is the one that will finally pay off—only to see little to no traction.

- **Negative feedback**

    I used to take criticism personally, but over time, I learned it's often the most honest advice you'll get. If customers repeatedly voice the same concerns, it's the market speaking.

- **Emotional toll**

    Building a business isn't just a financial commitment; it's a mental and physical one. The grind of those first six to twelve months can wear anyone down. If a venture constantly drains me without any sense of personal reward or purpose, I have to question why I'm still in it.

    But not all struggles are red flags. Take MrBeast, for example. This guy, one of YouTube's biggest names now, spent years creating daily content that went mostly ignored. His metrics were low, feedback was sparse, and his motivation dwindled. And yet he never quit. He spent months studying YouTube, analyzing filmmaking techniques and what videos went viral. And wouldn't you know it, before long, one of his videos blew up, setting the stage for everything he's built since. MrBeast's story illustrates the importance of resilience and reading red flags in context. His stagnant growth wasn't a sign to quit; it was a reason to refine, to keep going until his timing and content aligned with his audience. Sometimes, the breakthrough is right around the corner and you just have to keep pushing toward it.

In one of my early ventures, I had to leave money on the table—a frightening concept for any businessperson. In reality, walking away meant saving myself from deeper losses. Imagine you're running a business that loses $100 a day. Without an exit plan, you might stay the course, clinging to the hope that tomorrow will be different. But if you cut your losses on day four instead of day ten, you've saved $600. So, did you lose $400 or gain $600? That depends on how you look at it.

But exit strategies are not just for businesses that seem doomed. Even successful ventures can demand a strategic exit to protect your long-term goals. Take DJs, like the renowned Avicii, who had everything the world could offer—fame, money, private jets—but in the end, he didn't find enough lasting fulfillment to continue living. He was living a life that looked perfect on the surface, but there was a void, a lack of purpose beyond the status. This story serves as a powerful reminder that success without meaning can feel empty, and sticking to something that no longer brings value isn't worth the cost.

Maverick Takeaways

- Failure isn't a setback—it's an accelerator. The faster you fail, the faster you can learn and adjust your strategy.

- Success without failure is an illusion. Real growth comes from tough lessons that only failure can teach.

- Setbacks reveal the flaws in your approach. Every stumble is an opportunity to refine your method and emerge stronger.

- Celebrate failures as much as successes. They're just as essential in building resilience and shaping your business.

- Perfectionism is the enemy of progress. Trying to avoid failure often stalls your journey more than any setback ever could.

- The faster you fail, the quicker you reach your goal. Embracing failure allows you to make adjustments in real time, driving you closer to long-term success.

CHAPTER ELEVEN

Success Is the Easy Part

Conventional thought:
Success is the hard part.

Maverick truth: Staying successful is even harder.

The day I finally secured a contract with a high-profile tech company, I thought I had clinched the deal of a lifetime. It had taken months of hard work, negotiations, and countless pitches, but it was all worth it. This was the contract that would elevate my recruitment business to the next level, a deal that would prove my team's value and expertise in the industry. I leaned back for the first time in what felt like forever, allowing myself a moment of satisfaction. *We made it*, I thought.

But in business, comfort can be dangerous, and my brief moment of relief didn't last. Only a week later, my main contact at the company—the HR executive who'd championed the deal and believed in my vision—unexpectedly left her role. She was gone, and with her departure, everything we'd built over the past few months felt like it was slipping away. Suddenly, I found myself back at square one, facing a new HR head with a completely different vision and approach. It was like trying to sell the same idea to a stranger who hadn't been part of any of our previous discussions, who had no reason to trust us or understand the value we'd already proven.

In the weeks that followed, every meeting became a battle to resell the deal. The new HR lead was looking for something else entirely—he had his own agenda, his own milestones, and his own criteria for success. The resumes we'd meticulously selected to showcase our candidate pipeline now seemed irrelevant. The candidates we'd carefully aligned with the previous HR manager's vision no longer fit the bill. My team and I had spent weeks sourcing top talent, compiling twenty CVs to show the breadth and quality of our network, and now those CVs were just so much paper.

I realized that if we wanted to save this deal, we'd have to completely adapt to this new person's expectations. It wasn't enough to rely on the rapport we'd built with the last manager; we had to understand this new contact's mindset, his culture, and the kind of talent he valued. Was he looking for seasoned professionals with decades of experience? Or did he prefer young, dynamic talent willing to grow within the company? I had to figure this out quickly if I wanted any hope of salvaging the relationship.

And so, we went back to the drawing board, reassessing everything. I started by diversifying our candidate pool even further, sourcing profiles that aligned more closely with the new HR head's preferences. This meant reaching out to contacts all over the world, from India to China to the United States—not just relying on local talent. We scoured the industry, even approaching people who were already employed, to see if they might be open to a better offer—a company with better benefits, more upward mobility, a more compelling vision. We couldn't afford to give this guy any reason to look elsewhere.

On top of this, I had to establish a whole new relationship with him—one built from scratch. I needed him to see us as more than just another recruitment agency. We had to sell our value all over again, emphasizing how well we understood his company's needs and how we could tailor our approach to meet his goals. This wasn't just about finding candidates; it was about proving that we could help shape his team in a way that aligned with his vision.

> **I realized that success isn't a finish line; it's just the beginning of a different kind of challenge.**

But as the weeks dragged on, it became clear that he wasn't interested in carrying on the work his predecessor had started. Despite my best efforts, the deal was ultimately downsized to a fraction of its original value. All the time, energy, and resources we'd poured into securing that contract felt like a painful lesson in how volatile success can be. The financial loss hurt, but the lesson about the nature of success was even more valuable. I realized that success isn't a finish line; it's just the beginning of a different kind of challenge.

It was then that I understood a crucial principle: In business, you can never afford to sit in the passenger seat. Letting go of the wheel, even for a moment, can lead to a crash. Success requires relentless vigilance, constant adaptation, and an unyielding commitment to stay in control. I have to stay in the driver's seat, ready to steer through every twist and turn, ready to pivot whenever the road shifts unexpectedly.

> ## The Perils of Success Complacency
>
> Success often breeds a false sense of comfort, and that comfort can quickly turn into complacency. Complacency is a silent risk, creeping in when everything seems to be going smoothly, urging you to relax your standards and ease up on your efforts. But the truth is, comfort zones in business are dangerous places—they dull your instincts, slow down your response time, and make you vulnerable to change. One of the toughest lessons I've learned is that the minute you start feeling secure is the same minute you risk losing it all. Complacency blinds you to the shifting market forces, emerging competitors, and evolving client demands that are constantly in motion. It's like driving on cruise control without realizing the road is about to curve; if you don't take back control, you'll find yourself veering off course.

Success Is Not Security

As I learned, success can be fragile. Just one small shift—a change in leadership, a new direction from the client—was all it took to shake everything I thought I'd secured. I had to accept that in business, nothing is ever truly "done." Wins may open doors, but they also bring new challenges and risks that require constant vigilance.

The experience with the recruitment company taught me that success demands the same level of commitment and focus as the climb to get there, if not more. The higher you climb, the more people are watching, waiting to see if you'll slip up. Competitors are paying attention, ready to exploit any misstep. This is true in real estate, where once a sale falls through, the vultures are already circling overhead to swoop in and claim it for themselves. And it's true in any other type of business where clients who see your success and pay higher prices have higher expectations and are, therefore, less forgiving.

Success also changes the dynamics of your business. When you're an underdog, people might overlook your mistakes, but once you've made a name for yourself, every decision is scrutinized. You're expected to deliver at a higher standard consistently. There's no room for error, and there's certainly no space for resting on past achievements. If you're not evolving, if you're not constantly striving to stay ahead, you're already falling behind.

> **Staying successful means challenging your assumptions, questioning your strategies, and always looking for ways to improve.**

True success demands a growth mindset—a willingness to constantly learn, adapt, and expand your knowledge base, even when you're already at the top. People with a growth mindset don't view success as the finish line; instead, they treat it as the next step in a marathon. Staying successful means challenging your assumptions, questioning your strategies, and always looking for ways to improve. Many businesses fall into a pattern of stagnation once they reach a certain level, relying on the same strategies that brought them initial success. But in a world that's constantly evolving, those who cling to what worked in the past will be outpaced by those who are willing to change and innovate. The higher you rise, the stronger your commitment to growth must become. The moment you stop pushing forward, someone else is ready to take your place.

The lesson I learned—and one I want every entrepreneur to understand—is that success is not a destination; it's a challenge to keep raising your standards. It's easy to think you can coast once you reach a certain level, but that mindset is the quickest path to failure. Those who sustain success are the ones who stay hungry, who continue to operate with the same drive and vigilance that got them there in the first place. They know that reaching the top is only one part of the journey, and staying there requires a whole new level of dedication and adaptability.

> **Success is not a destination; it's a challenge to keep raising your standards.**

In the end, I realized that success is like holding water in your hands. It requires a constant, intentional effort to keep it from slipping through your fingers. Success may feel solid, but it's constantly shifting, and it challenges you to keep growing, keep pushing, and stay ahead of whatever comes next.

When you reach a milestone, consider it not as a place to rest but as a launching point for what comes next. Success should fuel your momentum, opening doors to new possibilities and helping you leverage past achievements to go even further. At every high point, ask yourself, "What can I do next? How can I take this momentum and apply it to a new challenge or opportunity?" This mindset transforms each success into a building block rather than a resting point. Treat every accomplishment as a call to go bigger, to explore new territories, and to refine your skills. Success isn't a reason to relax; it's the very reason to raise your standards, increase your resilience, and double down on your commitment to long-term growth.

When you've accomplished something big, it seems only natural to want to let down your guard a little and take your foot off the gas. But that feeling of security is a mirage. In business, there's no such thing as "safe" or "secure." The moment you think you're in control, circumstances shift, and suddenly you're scrambling to adapt. Now I use that moment of success as a checkpoint, a reminder to double down and assess what needs attention. I ask myself tough questions: "What weaknesses am I ignoring? Where am I assuming things are secure when they might not be? What blind spots could become risks if I'm not careful?" It's a practice of never assuming that the ground beneath me is stable just because I've reached a certain level.

Does that mean you should never enjoy your success? Absolutely not. Celebrate your wins, but don't let them fool you into thinking you can ease up. Every milestone is just another point where you need to refocus and recalibrate. Complacency leads to missed opportunities, strained client relationships, and, ultimately, decline. When you treat every success as the start of a new road to success, full of challenges of its own, you pave a highway that can take you further than you ever imagined.

Small Mistakes, Big Consequences

Success can unravel over the smallest mistakes. When I started pushing toward bigger goals, it was easy to focus only on the major moves—the bold decisions, the ambitious plans. But in reality, I've found it's often the little things, the details that seem almost trivial, that can make or break you. In high-stakes business, even the smallest oversight can set off a ripple effect, undermining everything you've worked for.

I'll admit, success has a way of making you feel invincible, like you can afford to be a little lax with the details. But I learned the hard way that's exactly when you need to be even more attentive. Once I hit a certain level, comfort started to creep in, and I found myself overlooking the same things that initially drove my success. In my experience, every small detail is a potential point of failure if neglected. Running a successful operation isn't just about making big, bold moves; it's about keeping everything—big and small—in check.

Here are five overlooked details I've learned to stay vigilant about:

1. Communication breakdown: Communication is the glue that holds my team together, but I'll be the first to admit it's easy to let it slip once you feel like you've "made it." I noticed that when we hit milestones, we'd ease up on regular check-ins, both internally and with clients. Without consistent communication, small misunderstandings quickly turn into bigger issues. I had to remind myself that keeping everyone in sync is essential, no matter how comfortable things seem.

2. Neglecting client relationships: It's easy to assume that a client is secure once a contract is signed. I've made that mistake too. But regular client check-ins are a powerful way to strengthen relationships and stay tuned into any shifts in their needs. I've lost clients by assuming everything was fine; maintaining trust is an ongoing effort. Now, I prioritize client relationships by keeping the lines of communication open and making sure my clients know their business is valued long after the ink is dry.

3. Overlooking employee well-being: My business depends on a motivated, healthy team. In my early days, I assumed that as long as work was getting done, everything was fine. But I quickly realized that people aren't machines and ignoring signs of burnout or stress only leads to lost productivity and high turnover. I now make it a point to check in with my team, knowing that looking out for their well-being isn't just good for them; it's essential for the health of the business.

4. Losing track of financial metrics: Before I make any big purchases, I set a simple rule: Only buy if I can comfortably afford to buy ten of them in cash without missing the money. This way, I stay in control of my spending, because I know even a million can disappear in the blink of an eye if you're not paying attention.

5. Resistance to adaptation: I've seen too many entrepreneurs cling to the saying "Don't change a running system." While there's wisdom there, today's world demands adaptability. Technology, trends, and markets are constantly shifting. Once people think they've "made it," they often stop looking for ways to improve or embrace new ideas. I've had to remind myself that no matter how successful I feel, there's always room to learn and grow. Now, I seek out workshops, networking events, and other entrepreneurs' perspectives to keep my mind open and my strategies fresh.

These five areas are the backbone of keeping success sustainable. I've come to view every part of my business as critical to the whole—no email is too trivial, no conversation too minor, and no feedback too inconsequential. Staying vigilant and paying attention to these "small" details has become my strategy for maintaining what I've built.

For anyone who's achieved a big milestone, my advice is this: Don't let the small stuff slide. Those seemingly minor details hold everything together, and they can be the difference between sustaining your success and watching it unravel. The smallest mistakes can lead to the biggest consequences, but with the right level of care, you can catch them before they turn into setbacks.

Success Maintenance Checklist

✓ **Assess your assumptions.**
Review recent achievements and ask, "Am I assuming any part of this is 'secure'?"

✓ **Implement a "small details" review system.**
Designate someone (or yourself) to double-check small, easy-to-overlook tasks: client follow-ups, feedback responses, staffing adjustments.

✓ **Reassess market positioning quarterly.**
Regularly review your market position and assess shifts in industry trends, competitor strategies, and customer preferences. Ask yourself: "Are we still aligned with the current market, or have we drifted?"

✓ **Strengthen key client relationships.**
Identify your top clients and proactively check in with them. Understand their evolving needs and priorities to ensure your offerings remain valuable. This keeps you ahead of potential issues and strengthens client loyalty.

✓ **Prioritize talent development.**
Invest in your team's growth by scheduling regular skill assessments, training, and development opportunities. A stronger team means a more resilient business that can adapt to changing demands and unexpected challenges.

✓ **Build a contingency strategy.**
Prepare for potential setbacks by developing a contingency plan for key areas of your business (e.g., client retention, revenue streams, staffing). This allows for quick pivots when conditions change unexpectedly.

✓ **Conduct regular "blind spot" audits.**
Engage a third party or trusted advisor to identify any blind spots you may have overlooked—areas where risks may be lurking. Regular external audits can highlight potential vulnerabilities before they turn into issues.

Adaptability: The Only Constant in Success

One of the most crucial lessons I've learned in business is that adaptability is the backbone of sustained success. It's easy to think that once you've achieved something big, you've found a formula you can rely on. But in reality, the landscape is always shifting, and what worked yesterday may not work tomorrow. To hold on to success, you have to stay nimble, ready to adjust your strategy, your perspective, and sometimes even your goals to keep pace with change.

After my experience with the recruitment contract, I understood that flexibility was essential. Securing that deal felt like a huge victory, but when my main point of contact left, I had to start over with someone who had a completely different vision. If I'd been rigid in my approach, insisting on the exact terms of the original contract, I would have lost the client entirely. Instead, I had to adapt quickly, reframe my pitch, and find new ways to meet their evolving needs. That pivot required humility and a willingness to let go of my initial expectations. It was uncomfortable, but it taught me that adaptability is a skill every entrepreneur must master if they want their success to last.

Adaptability means more than just responding to challenges; it's about anticipating changes and being proactive in your approach. In business, waiting until you're forced to adapt can be costly. Instead, I look ahead, assessing trends in my industry and in my clients' businesses, asking myself where I might need to pivot before circumstances make it a necessity, because acting is so much more powerful than reacting. Every few months, I take stock of what's working and what isn't and what adjustments I can make to stay relevant and effective.

Adaptability isn't just about reacting to change—it's about creating an organizational culture that thrives on agility and innovation. To sustain success, adaptability must become part of your team's DNA, a core value that everyone understands and practices. By encouraging a culture where experimentation is valued and failure is seen as a learning tool rather than a setback, you create an environment where people aren't afraid to pivot, test new ideas, and challenge assumptions. I make it a point to reward creative problem-solving and proactive thinking, because those traits are what keep us on the cutting edge. Adaptability is not a solo endeavor; it's a collective mindset that everyone in the business contributes to. When the entire team is conditioned to expect and embrace change, it becomes easier to seize new opportunities and pivot when challenges arise.

> **To sustain success, adaptability must become part of your team's DNA, a core value that everyone understands and practices.**

Flexibility doesn't mean compromising your core values or vision—it's about adjusting the methods to achieve them. For example, when I face changes in my contracts, I keep my goal of delivering high-value services front and center, even if the approach has to shift. That focus allows me to stay adaptable without losing sight of what really matters. And when you're willing to experiment with new methods, test out fresh ideas, or shift your approach, you discover strategies that might never have surfaced if you'd stuck rigidly to what's familiar.

Sometimes, adaptability means facing setbacks head-on and transforming them into strategic pivots. I've encountered moments when an initial plan fell apart, but instead of seeing it as a failure, I looked for ways to reframe it as an opportunity. For instance, after a client contract fell through, I analyzed what went wrong and used that insight to create an improved approach that ultimately attracted new clients. When you approach setbacks with a mindset of growth, each obstacle becomes a chance to refine your strategy, expand your knowledge, and build resilience. Adapting in the face of failure isn't just survival—it's an opportunity to strengthen your foundation and emerge stronger.

Bottom line for any entrepreneur: Adaptability is your best insurance against becoming outdated or irrelevant. The world moves quickly, and those who hold too tightly to a single way of doing things often find themselves left behind.

> **Adaptability is your best insurance against becoming outdated or irrelevant. The world moves quickly, and those who hold too tightly to a single way of doing things often find themselves left behind.**

Vision, Values, and Team Culture: Building Lasting Success

One of the most valuable lessons I've learned is that the best teams are those where every individual feels a sense of ownership and purpose. When team members see themselves as stakeholders in the mission, they bring passion and initiative that can't be manufactured or imposed. To foster this, I work to create an environment where everyone has a voice, where ideas are shared freely, and where each person feels connected to the success of the whole. When people feel empowered and know that their contributions matter, they're more willing to go the extra mile, take on responsibility, and hold themselves accountable. By building a culture of ownership, you're not just creating a team—you're creating a legacy of commitment and drive that extends beyond any single project or quarter.

I learned firsthand the cost of being overlooked and overworked when I was running that Burger King station at the airport that typically required three people. Day after day, I worked myself to the bone, sweating up a storm and handling everything solo just to make things run smoothly. I was saving my employer money, doing the work of three people for the price of one, and yet, when I requested a raise, my efforts were ignored. I wasn't asking for a handout—I just wanted recognition for the dedication I was putting in, the sacrifices I was making to keep that place running. But all I got was silence. It's a feeling I'll never forget.

Now, as a leader, I make it a priority to check in with my team regularly to ensure they don't feel the way I did back then. I want them to know they're valued, their hard work matters, and going above and beyond won't go unnoticed. When someone stays late, brings fresh ideas, or puts in the extra effort, I make sure they know it counts, recognizing that dedication not only keeps morale high but also keeps people invested in the vision we're building together.

Client relationships also need consistent nurturing. Once a partnership is established, it's easy to assume it will continue running smoothly. But every relationship requires regular engagement, communication, and reinforcement to stay strong. I learned this lesson the hard way when I lost a key client due to neglecting these basics. Since then, I've made a point of keeping open lines of communication and making every client feel valued.

No matter how many clients you secure or how long they've been with you, treating each one as if they're your first is critical to maintaining strong relationships. I've made it a point to keep communication personalized, making clients feel valued as unique partners rather than just accounts on a roster. In my experience, clients sense when they're being taken for granted, and that's often the beginning of the end of a partnership. I ensure that we tailor our approaches to meet their evolving needs, celebrate their milestones with them, and stay invested in their growth. This approach isn't just good for client retention—it builds loyalty, trust, and a reputation for excellence that can open doors to new opportunities.

Finally, maintaining a solid communication structure within the team is crucial, especially as your business scales. When we were a small team, everyone could reach me directly. But as we expanded, that became unsustainable. Now we have a clear structure in place where each group has a leader to report to, and issues are escalated as needed. This ensures that every team member's voice is heard and critical concerns are addressed.

Building a Sustainable Financial Strategy

Financial success doesn't just demand careful spending; it requires a proactive, strategic approach to growth. One of the biggest shifts I've made in my approach to financial discipline is treating each success as a resource to fuel future gains, not as a reward in itself. I reinvest in areas that will yield long-term benefits, like team development, innovative tools, and market research. Instead of splurging on short-term luxuries, I've learned to prioritize investments that will strengthen our core capabilities and expand our reach. Financial discipline is about creating a growth cycle, where each gain fuels the next initiative, allowing the business to thrive in a sustainable way. It's a balance between enjoying the rewards of hard work and ensuring that each dollar works to secure our future.

After a few early wins, I found myself tempted to make bold moves—upgrades, flashy purchases, and expansions that, in hindsight, were more about feeding my ego than growing my business. The thrill of success had made me feel invincible, and that illusion of security led me to make financial decisions I would later regret. Success has a way of making you believe that the money will always be there, but the truth is nothing in business is guaranteed. That experience taught me the value of financial discipline: to think beyond the immediate gain and plan for sustainability.

> **Financial success doesn't just demand careful spending; it requires a proactive, strategic approach to growth.**

Over time, I developed a set of financial practices that became the backbone of my business stability. I learned to set aside reserves, establish clear budgets, and evaluate each spending decision in the context of long-term growth rather than short-term satisfaction. For any entrepreneur, financial discipline is the bridge between success and longevity. It's the quiet work that often goes unnoticed but makes all the difference when things get tough. It's about recognizing that success today doesn't guarantee success tomorrow unless you manage your resources wisely. By treating each dollar as an investment in the future, you build a foundation that can withstand the ups and downs of the business world, ensuring that your hard-earned success doesn't slip away with one impulsive decision.

> **For any entrepreneur, financial discipline is the bridge between success and longevity.**

Success often brings new costs—scaling up means bigger payrolls, more office space, and increased operational expenses. One of the hardest lessons I had to learn was recognizing the hidden costs that come with growth and the importance of preparing for them. Early on, I underestimated these costs and faced cash flow issues that could have been avoided with better planning. Now I make it a habit to forecast expenses that come with each growth milestone and set aside reserves specifically for unexpected costs. Success isn't just about increasing revenue; it's about carefully managing the expenses that come along for the ride. By planning for these hidden costs, you're able to scale responsibly without jeopardizing the financial stability of the business.

As I look back on everything I've shared in these chapters, I'm reminded that success is never a single moment, a one-time achievement, or a final destination; it's a living, breathing journey—a continuous process that requires commitment, humility, and a willingness to grow. Every lesson, from embracing failure to nurturing team culture and maintaining financial discipline, has taught me that success is both fragile and resilient. It's fragile when neglected but resilient when sustained with care, adaptability, and a relentless drive to improve.

In the end, building something that lasts isn't about reaching a milestone and stopping. It's about setting a foundation, learning from every experience, and choosing to push forward no matter the obstacles. Success is simply the beginning; it's what we do with it that determines whether it fades or transforms into something enduring. As you close this chapter, consider this your invitation to turn your own achievements into a legacy—one built on strength, intention, and impact.

Success is simply the beginning; it's what we do with it that determines whether it fades or transforms into something enduring.

Maverick Takeaways

- Success breeds complacency—if you let it. The real work begins once you've reached your goal; staying vigilant is essential.

- Small mistakes can undo big wins. In business, ignoring the minor details is often what derails even the best-laid plans.

- Holding on to success demands flexibility. Stubbornly clinging to past strategies is a surefire way to undermine your future.

- Achieving success is a sprint; maintaining it is a marathon. The real challenge is keeping success alive through ongoing effort.

- The details matter more at the top. When you reach success, every small oversight is magnified, so every action counts.

- Financial discipline is your true safety net. Flashy wins are meaningless without the foundational discipline to sustain them.

Conclusion

As you close this book, don't see it as the conclusion of your journey—see it as the beginning of something transformative. Every principle, every story, and every hard truth shared here were chosen to equip you with more than just practical knowledge; they were designed to instill a mindset that breaks free from conventional business wisdom. This journey isn't only about building a profitable venture; it's about creating a legacy on your terms—a legacy that reflects a vision, values, and an audacity to see the world differently.

Today's world is changing at lightning speed, and with that change comes an opening for entrepreneurs like you: those who think independently, refuse to settle for the predictable, and aren't afraid to question, innovate, and lead. The future needs leaders who will break the mold, who see success as an opportunity to make a difference, not just a bottom line. You're stepping into a space that rewards resilience, courage, and a fierce commitment to challenging outdated assumptions.

The contrarian mindset isn't just another tool in your tool kit; it's the foundation of what will set you apart. It's what will keep you pushing forward when others are retreating and what will anchor you to your mission when the road gets hard. Remember, achieving success is only a single chapter—the real story lies in how you sustain it, evolve it, and use it to create an impact that transcends profit margins or fleeting recognition.

From this point on, ask yourself the real questions: Are you willing to stand by your principles when they're tested? Are you prepared to pivot boldly, even when it feels uncertain? Will you see failure not as a setback but as the bedrock for your next achievement? The path ahead is not easy, and it's not for everyone. But that's what makes it extraordinary.

Don't be afraid to lead with your values. In a world that so often glorifies shortcuts and compromise, you have the opportunity to create something rooted in purpose and integrity. Build a team that shares your vision and holds you accountable to it, challenges you, and rises and falls with you. A great team isn't just an asset; it's the unbreakable core that will see you through every triumph and every trial.

Conventional wisdom will urge you to stay safe, to follow a familiar path, to keep your head down. But you know as well as I do that greatness isn't found on well-worn trails. It's found in the willingness to risk, to stand firm in your convictions, and to continue long after others have quit. Let this mindset be your edge, your armor, and your compass as you step into new, uncharted terrain.

Imagine the impact you could make—not just on your business, but on the world around you. Think about the legacy you're building, the lives you're influencing, and the standards you're setting. This isn't just about financial success; it's about creating something that embodies who you are and what you believe. In doing so, you're not just preparing for the future—you're actively shaping it.

> **Go forward with this mindset, and you won't just build a business—you'll build a legacy.**

Take the contrarian mindset and make it your own. Question what others take for granted. Challenge assumptions. Stay bold, stay curious, and stay driven by purpose. The future belongs to those who are willing to push beyond the limits, to innovate not only for profit but for meaning. This journey is yours to define. Step forward with conviction, with courage, and with the knowledge that you already have everything you need—not by following someone else's blueprint, but by designing your own.

Go forward with this mindset, and you won't just build a business—you'll build a legacy.

Now it's time to take everything you've read, everything you've absorbed, and put it into action. The world will not wait for you to get ready, and neither should you. So today—yes, today—take one step that will move you toward your boldest dream, your most daring vision. Whether it's a small change, a big leap, or something in between, make it happen. Let the contrarian mindset you've learned be your guide, and remember—action is what turns ideas into legacies.

Reflection Questions

20 Questions to Compare Conventional Thought Versus Maverick Truth

1. What belief or assumption have I always accepted as true but may be limiting my success?
2. In what ways am I still following the crowd instead of forging my own path?
3. When was the last time I challenged my own thinking?
4. What's a risk I've avoided out of fear, and what would happen if I took that leap?
5. How often do I listen to my own intuition versus relying on the advice of others?
6. In which areas of my business or life am I settling for "good enough"?
7. What could happen if I stopped playing it safe?
8. Am I making decisions based on long-term growth or short-term comfort?
9. What's one "failure" I've had that, in hindsight, could be reframed as a valuable lesson?

10. Where am I afraid of success or growth?
11. How much of my current business strategy was influenced by industry norms, and could I approach it differently?
12. What would happen if I took full responsibility for both my successes and my failures?
13. What would I do if I knew I could not fail?
14. How could I turn my biggest obstacle into an opportunity?
15. Where am I staying loyal to people or methods that aren't serving my vision anymore?
16. What's one unconventional move I can make today to jump-start my next phase of success?
17. How can I use my perceived weaknesses as a strength?
18. What limiting beliefs do I have about money, success, and failure?
19. How does the conventional view of "work-life balance" influence my business decisions?
20. Where do I need to let go of outdated strategies and be more adaptable?

Questions to Enhance Readers' Courage and Push Beyond Fear

1. What's the worst-case scenario if I fail? Is that worse than never trying?
2. How will I feel a year from now if I don't take action today?
3. What is the one thing I'm terrified of doing that I know would dramatically change my life if I did it?

4. What would I do if I knew I couldn't fail?
5. What small step can I take today to get closer to a goal I've been avoiding?
6. How often am I making decisions based on fear instead of potential?
7. What would I tell my younger self about not letting fear hold me back?
8. What's stopping me from taking action—other people or my own fears?
9. What would I do if I wasn't afraid of being judged?
10. What would my future self thank me for doing today?
11. Where am I holding on to comfort, and how is that limiting my growth?
12. What's one decision I've been avoiding that, if I made it, would change everything?
13. What's the most daring decision I've ever made, and how did it pay off?
14. What would I do if I had complete belief in my abilities?
15. What action will I take today, even if I'm scared?
16. Who do I need to become in order to handle the next level of success?
17. How can I change my relationship with fear to make it work for me, not against me?
18. What's one thing I know I should do but haven't because I'm afraid?
19. What would happen if I embraced failure as part of my growth process instead of something to avoid?

Bonus: Deep Self-Reflection Questions

1. What kind of legacy do I want to leave with my business?
2. How am I aligning my business with my personal values?
3. How can I build a business that will thrive, not just survive?
4. What does true success look like to me?
5. How do I want to be remembered in the business world, and what am I doing to earn that reputation?
6. What areas of my life do I need to take more ownership of?
7. What's one thing I've been putting off because I think it's too risky?
8. How am I intentionally shaping my business culture?
9. What's a new belief I want to adopt to accelerate my growth?

Acknowledgments

I'd like to acknowledge the ones who doubted me, rejected me, or failed to see my potential. You are the reason I am who I am today. Every setback was a lesson, every rejection was fuel for my fire. Your disbelief only pushed me to prove that a Maverick never follows the crowd. To those who didn't trust my vision, thank you for unknowingly sharpening my resolve and inspiring me to build my own path.

About the Author

Dr. Reza Zahedi's journey is one of transformation, resilience, and unwavering determination. Having fled Iran as a child, Reza overcame adversity and seized opportunities against all odds. At just twenty years old, while studying civil engineering, he took a leap of faith and launched a nightclub chain, marking the beginning of a multifaceted entrepreneurial journey that would span across industries and continents.

But Reza's story isn't just about business—it's about mindset. Early on, he learned that success isn't handed to you; it's earned through grit, perseverance, and the courage to defy the norm. One pivotal moment in his life came when he was facing a difficult crossroads, deciding whether to take a stable corporate job or risk it all to follow his passion. Reza chose the latter, and it paid off—leading him to real estate, where he expanded his company across China and the United States, and solidifying his reputation as a globally recognized entrepreneur.

In 2024, Reza founded Leadtainment, a revolutionary platform designed to mentor and empower entrepreneurs. Through transformative events and a network of like-minded leaders, Leadtainment enables the next generation to break barriers and achieve lasting success, just as Reza did.

Armed with a PhD in civil engineering, Reza's expertise stretches beyond traditional business. His true strength lies in his ability to turn bold ideas into tangible results. Whether he's navigating the complexities of real estate or developing innovative ways to empower others, his approach is always rooted in vision, purpose, and the relentless pursuit of growth.

Reza's mission is clear: to inspire entrepreneurs to think bigger, embrace challenges, and create businesses that stand the test of time. His story proves that no matter where you start, your potential is limitless if you refuse to give up and remain true to your vision.